THE BENEFIT
OF THE EX

The Benefit of the Ex

Making Love Visible When Everything Changes

June Dillinger

Published by June Dillinger

(808) 330-5555
Email: info@makinglovevisible.com
https://makinglovevisible.com/

Edited by Duane Lee with The Infinite Writer Agency, LLC
Cover Art by Mark Dillinger, Dillinger Arts and Design by Grace Manser
Book Design by Tamara Cribley, The Deliberate Page
Final Copy Check by Margaret V. Herrick

Note: The information presented in this book is for professional, personal, and
self-development purposes only. The author is not counseling, acting as a therapist,
psychologist, or any mental health physician on the reader's behalf. Reader should
consult a licensed mental health physician for mental health diagnosis and solutions.
The author is not liable for how readers may choose to use this information.

Library of Congress Cataloguing in Publication Data
Dillinger, June

The Benefit of the Ex: Making Love Visible When Everything Changes

First Printing 2020
ISBN 978-0-578-62003-9

This book is dedicated to my family and friends who never thought they'd ever hear me say, "It's done!" I thank them for the endless support and belief that they placed in me and within this body of work. I am deeply thankful for Raymond Woo, my former husband of nearly two decades, for giving me the thumbs up when I first mentioned the idea to him. He supported the plan from its inception and lovingly told me, "June, you can take this all the way to Oprah!"

This book is also dedicated to my son, Macklin, who has endured split parents and, at the same time, has loved each of us equally and grown into a balanced young man. Macklin somehow made room for each of us to become who we needed to be. His support is all I could have ever wanted!

I recall my first encounter with B. Kenneth McGee who wrote the book *Eyes Wide Shut*. Like a father, Kenny became my confidant and angel, listening to me complain and grow over the years, and he never stopped encouraging me to share this gift. For his constant love, I am beyond grateful! While he is no longer living, his memory lives on.

Finally, I'd like to acknowledge the God within me that said, "This is yours to do." Letting my Spirit be my guide as my true source. I am eternally grateful!

ACKNOWLEDGEMENTS

My colleague and friend, Chet Turnbeaugh, worked tirelessly blending my work for two intense years, bringing together a clear foundation for this book. No words can express my gratitude.

I'd like to acknowledge the writers who risked having their heartstrings snapped as they laid down their words that helped to heal themselves and support this book. My readers, Heather Bowles, Bryan Toda, and Shaye Maeda, who supported the book's direction by delving into over fifty stories to select the ones that best fit the book's criteria.

I'd like to acknowledge my dear friend, Ingrid R. Lewis, for her editing acumen, especially her ability to "weed out" my June-isms.

Thank you to Jasmine Skurtu and Caroline Groppe who all braved the entire manuscript, offering their thoughts and said *"yes!"* with their conscious comments.

It is with great respect for the craft and trade of an author that I honor Hawaiian, Mahealani Harris whose feedback opened a window to my final decision on how my book should be presented and shared. She clarified a turning point for me that I cannot be thankful enough for.

I have a dear appreciation for Writing Coach Patrick Snow and friend Rose Suemoto, the first two who walked with me through the two bodies of work I created and did their best to offer me their endless guidance and coaching.

I also want to acknowledge Sharon Akaki, my friend that kept asking "when" because I knew it was about keeping my word to myself. Sharon supported my choices, thank God!

Mark Dillinger (DillingerArts.com), my brother, painter and graphic artist, carefully designed the cover of this book with his expert eye, taking my ideas and feedback with immense patience. Grace Manser fine-tuned the content of the cover and branding effect. Dating back to the beginning, it was Ed Baker III whose tireless support helped with all my original graphics with x's, butterflies and swirls. Without these beloved souls who believed in me and this book, I would not have the platform to move forward. *Making Love Visible* became possible because of their commitment to help me see it through.

Joanie Winberg, divorce mentor and facilitator, must be mentioned. She kept me in her loop since the inception of my idea. Deep gratitude for her continued work exists!

Last but certainly not least, I'd like to thank, Roger Jellinek, the agent who first heard my idea publicly, thirteen years ago, and said, "This is good," and I believed him. Thank you, Roger!

And to all of those I may have missed (over a decade is a long time to be working on this "masterpiece"), your grace and your care became a vibration and a part of this book. Thank you. You gave me light to carry on.

PRAISE FOR *THE BENEFIT OF THE EX*

"We were born to swim in love, drink in love, laugh and play in love. Love is the current and currency of the universe. June Dillinger explains how in times of stress and loss—like ex, for example—love is the answer. It's love that heals our wounds, eliminates needless suffering, and gives us the happiness we need and want. June will guide you beautifully in that process."

Greg Baer
Author *Real Love*

"This is a book so filled with interesting and wise observations about life events we all experience. It made me think about things I've been through in a totally different way, giving me perspectives about my life events which were revelatory. For the better. I started planning to read it again as soon as I finished it. Thank you, June."

Angelo Pizzo
American Screenwriter/Film Producer *Hoosiers* and *Rudy*

"June reminds us that when we love, accept, and forgive ourselves, we are *free*— free to love, accept, and forgive others; free to get past our pain; free to make our love visible; and free to experience life in exciting and profound ways that we never dreamed possible."

Dr. Kent M. Keith
Author, *Anyway: The Paradoxical Commandments*

"Change disrupts our usual way of being and surrendering what was familiar can be a very tough situation that is extremely challenging for many of us. *The Benefit of the Ex* guides the reader on a journey to the love deep within and prepares the heart and mind for a greater expression of that love. Thank you, Ms. June Dillinger, for this honest, phenomenal book that shows us how to let go, and then... how to receive so much more than we ever thought was possible."

Rickie Byars
Director of Music & Arts, Agape Int'l
Spiritual Center Los Angeles, CA

"June's advice is solid. As someone who has many exes, I've learned not to blame in shame, but letting go of love is always the answer."

Judy Carter
America's Funniest Motivational Speaker,
Stress Reduction Expert/Humorist

"June clearly shows in the masterful pages that follow how your past does not have to determine who you are today, but how your thoughts today can certainly impact your new reality and destiny tomorrow. She also shows you how to love yourself in a whole and complete new way, so you can live a rich, fulfilling, and more worthwhile life."

Dr. John Demartini
International Bestselling Author, *The Values Factor*

TABLE OF CONTENTS

FOREWORD

Junie, as we affectionately called her growing up together in a sunny, Southern Californian cul-de-sac on the hill, was *the girl I wanted to be*. This will be news to her as she reads this for the first time. Throughout grade school, which was conveniently located right across the street, I felt like an outsider. It was hard to escape my geeky persona with daily reminders from classmates of my "flat face" and "*chink* eyes," or being called a "four-eyed *gook*," when I finally got fitted for glasses. Having to defend the pungent cooking smells (most likely my father's favorite tripe soup) wafting across the street from the only Korean home on the block, sealed my fate as *other*.

Although she was the cooler, prettier elder *statesman* (by a whopping two years), Junie was the only person who really *saw* me. To this shy eight-year-old girl, it was astounding that she chose to play with me, to make lunch for me, and to share her gorgeous wardrobe with me. Junie saw me.

Decades later, and thousands of miles apart, June in Honolulu, and myself in New York, we finally reconnected. Ironically, it was right after my grueling ten-year marriage ended that I reunited with Junie on a visit back to the old neighborhood. It was easy to share my feelings of hurt, disappointment, and a fear of starting over because I knew she had made it through her own marital breakup. But while I was still burdened by resentment and betrayal towards my ex and hampered by my new role as a victim, Junie seemed at peace. Somehow, she found a way to reclaim her love and become friends with her ex. Yes, you heard that right. Did she discover the holy grail of healing relationships? I wanted whatever she was having.

It is no coincidence that Junie is a leading wedding purveyor in Hawaii, hosted a cable TV show called *It's All About Love* for nine years, was the youth leader at Unity Church of Hawaii, and continues to celebrate the healing powers of what love can add to our lives. But this is not to say Junie's faith in love was not

1

tested time and time again. I remember the heavy day she found out that she was adopted. I remember when her adopted father, who was a paraplegic, was in the middle of a heated divorce with her mother when she learned her biological parents were other people. Still, I remember how Junie cared for him with tenderness and devotion for several years after that until he passed away. And most recently Junie, with an open heart, went on an emotional quest to find and reunite with her birth mother, despite the fear, betrayal, and pain that facing the unknown could have caused her. Without expectation, Junie's only intention was to thank this woman and let her know that she has lived a beautiful life. Now, Junie is a welcomed member of this woman's family, and a beloved daughter. Junie is love.

After a decade working as a TV producer for the Oprah Show, interviewing some of the world's foremost healers and leaders of social change, I have seen few people in my experience as dedicated to spreading love and beauty in the world as June Dillinger. Her desire to love and be loved and to help others to know that they matter is the glue that binds us, as friends, as colleagues, and as two women who have gone through hell and back to find the benefits of their exes. *The Benefit of the Ex* is a spiritual manual on how to forgive and manifest love throughout our lives, even with the person we call an ex. I don't know anyone more capable of helping you to learn these difficult lessons than June.

Janet Lee

Emmy Award-Winning Producer, Oprah Show / Author

Preface

"Kuleana," A TED Talk in the Making: "Ideas Worth Spreading"

On her website, the author of *Managing with Aloha*, Rosa Say, poignantly writes:

> *"Kuleana is one's personal sense of responsibility. The person possessing kuleana believes in the strength of this value and will be quick to say, "I accept my responsibilities, and I will be held accountable." Kuleana speaks the workplace language of self-motivation, ownership, empowerment, and the personal transformation, which can result from our hard work. Effective delegation becomes about the sharing of kuleana with others, recognizing where it rightfully belongs, or where it can facilitate hands-on learning. Kuleana can give us amazing clarity about what begins and ends with us as individuals. It will also give us a brutally honest clarity about our expectations of others: Are those expectations reasonable or not?"*

This book, *The Benefit of the Ex: Making Love Visible When Everything Changes*, has gone through some serious revisions, multiple drafts, and changes from its inception through to its completion. It took me nearly a decade to compile the information; teetering back-and-forth between ditching the idea, to the realization that it had tremendous worth. With the endless support and love from friends who kept asking me about it, I was finally able to finish this book and breathe new life into a decade-old project. Love took its needed time! I share this with you in part because I felt it was my kuleana to complete this work. As Rosa suggests, we all must face our responsibilities and encourage others to do the same. In creating this book, I was inspired to help others.

3

As time wore on, I knew that other people needed to find the same peace and abundance that I had found. From this place, came clarity and greater attention to the multiple ways this book could be used as a tool for positive transformation. There was a time I didn't celebrate my present, but through constant dedication and trust in the Universe, I was able to enjoy a richer life experience than I ever thought possible.

COURAGE, GRIT, AND BELIEF

My journey began when I wrote about my divorce, which inspired me to gather similar stories from others. I turned to the press, the media, and to the Internet to find people who felt called to share. I received dozens of stories all based on a single set of criteria that I hoped would help both the writers and their future readers. I've laid out what I wrote so many years ago to help you make sense of the context for the six stories that are found in the chapters that follow.

Once I had collected just over fifty stories, I stopped taking submissions. Next, I asked a few people from the community, each of whom had different relationship backgrounds, to read through all the stories and help me select the best ones. Each reader was asked to score the stories based on meeting the requested criteria. Fourteen stories were chosen. I set the project aside for four years before picking it up again and with more life experience under my belt. Plus, I didn't want to give up on something I knew the world needed.

A Note on the Personal Spirituality Contained in this Book

My experience with religion, as a child in a large Methodist church Sunday school, was usually having fun while my Mom was busy singing in the choir in the sanctuary. Years of similar formal religion followed me into my adolescence. Upon my move to Hawaii, I stepped away from the church.

My father moved to Oahu in his later years to be closer to me and just after his passing, some of our very good friends introduced me to Unity (a non-denominational church). It had been over 20 years since I'd stepped foot in a church, and it was the last thing I wanted to do. They told me they loved and trusted my father and that they also loved me. Finally, they talked me into joining them for a Sunday service.

I was moved by their request, and I decided to try it out—just once—out of respect for my father. What I discovered was both enchanting and painful. As I grew to understand more about myself, my world began to change. Because of what Unity had to offer, I later became a Licensed Unity Teacher, a role that gave me the opportunity to be a leader within the Unity community. Throughout the book, you will find sprinklings of my truth and understanding of spirituality. You can choose to incorporate these aspects into your life, or not. It is entirely your choice. I personally believe that all roads lead to the same path, including the one that you are on right now.

With infinite love,
June Dillinger

INTRODUCTION

"For the things we have to learn before we can do them, we learn by doing them." - Aristotle

To get the best use out of this book, it is recommended that you look carefully at your weaknesses or anything about yourself or life you would like to improve. Throughout this book, there will be a series of exercises shared as invitations that will facilitate your growth and development. You may complete them whenever you like, in any order that you like, if you like. They are an "invitation" to grow and thrive richly from the experience each creates in your life if you so wish.

Knowledge is the primary goal of non-fiction reading, yet the application of that knowledge is where change is born. It's one thing to be able to recite a line from a famous book; it's quite another to be able to act on its implications and navigate your life based on its meaning.

I hope the content here will offer tools that provide a source for learning, practicality, and application. It is only through doing that we learn to do that which we don't know how to do. To find new results, I ask that you have the courage to try something that might seem a little out of the ordinary.

THIS BOOK IS FOR YOU...

- if you are ready to accept responsibility for your life.

- if you want to be happy, and not remain right.

- if you are ready to start the rewarding work of letting Love have its way with your life.

7

CHAPTER 1

Opening Up for More

"The two most important days in your life are the day you are born and the day you find out why." - Mark Twain

As you read through these pages you will discover the divine surprise is you—all of you. Overcoming heartbreak is hard, especially when your mind wrestles with your heart. The biggest hurdle to overcome is convincing yourself that there are no more broken pieces left to clean up. Once you've freed your mind of the pain, your heart can fully open up to do the work, starting with conscious divorce, which I will explain in a moment.

To do this, you are going to have to learn how to see the benefits of your past experiences. Until you accept the past, you can't fully forgive yourself for the pain that you've experienced. One thing is for sure: There's no going back.

Consequently, the secret is to understand that you did these things to find and experience love. If you realize that, then you will come out of this more in love with yourself than you ever were before. Additionally, you will develop a mindset that cultivates success.

The question must now become this: Do you continue doing the same things that you've always done, or do you move on and use this hurt as a platform for allowing yourself to trust the process of growth? The greatest difficulty is processing our inner pain and dealing with it in a constructive way.

At some point in your life you may have seen a magic show, either in-person or on TV. In the performance, you also probably picked up on how a great magician can surprise the audience by doing something that is unthinkable. For instance, the famous magician, Harry Houdini, was known for his incredible escapes, though many left him injured or nearly killed. In other words, no one ever truly knows what will work itself out, but, as if by magic, one is always surprised when one's plans unfold in one's favor.

This may sound cavalier, or even uncaring, so before I put my foot in my mouth and say something as difficult as suggesting that you need to love yourself—understand this: The only person you need to heal is you. Divorcing yourself from any opposing situation may feel like the most painful journey you've ever been on. Even if you aren't in an actual divorce, it may feel as if your life itself is being uprooted. There is not a single person who has not felt some level of loss of a relationship, an opportunity, or even when one transitions from one stage in life to the next; a person tends to not want to leave one's comfort zone.

When I opened up to myself, I learned to love myself. It was difficult. I experienced just about every emotional setback (and triumph) to become the person I am today. My wish for you, by the time you finish reading this book, is that you will meet yourself in the mirror and discover your true self, your true beauty.

CONSCIOUS DIVORCE

Sometimes you have got to make deliberate choices that impact others. Conscious divorce is a topic that can occur in any area of your life. Unlike regular divorce, a conscious divorce is a proclamation that a person, thing, action, habit, or belief no longer serves you. To improve your own life, you must move forward and choose to divorce yourself from that which you no longer need.

Conscious divorce isn't just the decision to cut people or things out of your life. It is also a step towards accepting the beauty that these decisions can grant both parties. For example, perhaps your former partner has found the love of their life. Or, perhaps you have gained some clarity on your own life through the pain that you felt an ex-lover caused. These experiences can be healing because they make you feel, which causes us to examine our lives more closely.

In my own journey, I became more aware of who I was and began questioning myself much deeper after my divorce. Consciously separating means that you must drop the hatred, the fear, and get rid of the excuses. Instead, you have got to work towards creating the life you want and learn how to love yourself in the aftermath. Now, sometimes you will need to deliberately separate yourself from your past, as is the case with addictions, or any type of memories that are holding you back. You are not your past.

The important thing to remember is that everything with which you identify, associate with, or believe in is a relationship. You have a relationship with your personality, with your family, and with your choices. No matter what type of changes you are trying to make in your personal life, the relationships you have with all these aspects of your life can either hold you back or spring you forward.

RECEIVING THE BENEFIT: JUNE'S *"EXPERIENCE"*

Seeing the good that comes after two mutual parties decide to cut the knot is the *only* way to leave with your half of the rope still intact. To give you a sense of what this can look like, I still talk with my former husband, Ray. I don't regret any of the time that I spent with him, and to this day, we communicate, discussing topics about our son and, on occasion, other things as well. As a matter-of-fact, my ex is remarried, and his wife sings for my wedding business when she is available. In truth, at first, my friendship with them was not easy. Yet, it was precisely what I needed to become a better person. The only thing that got me through was knowing the following truth: Good can come from this! In fact, it's all part of the equation.

All things considered: This has been an incredibly challenging on-going process. There are still days where I get caught up in a romantic memory. I have even told my son that maybe his father and I will end up back together when we are in our nineties—who knows? However, what I have today, in my now moment, is all that really matters, and it's the only thing that I have any shred of control over. *This is the truth.*

I was living life—tending to my Dachshunds, Buddy of Beretania and Hoku, and enjoying the perks of living a mere two miles from the ocean in Hawaii, when I felt called to greater service. It began one day when my ex came by to drop off his monthly support check. When I accepted the check, I saw that it was more than the usual amount. I replied in a rather catty tone (while secretly being grateful): "There are so many benefits to an ex."

Thinking of just the money, it was an embarrassing remark that I actually spoke out loud.

However, I felt a strange sensation wash over me after the words were out in the open. I managed to follow up my thoughtless remark with a very sincere "thank you" on behalf of the fact that I needed the money. Yet, as the words came out, they changed me somehow, and it wasn't just the amount written on the check; I also recognized that by expressing gratitude, I felt a sensation of authenticity that hadn't been present between us for a very long time. I knew that my life was about to change—and I was ready to make that change.

Beaming with this newfound sense of gratitude, I told Ray that maybe I would write a book someday and title it *The Benefit of the Ex*. It would be about all the good that I had learned on my journey after our divorce. Ray grinned and told me that I could take my idea all the way to Oprah. It was the beginning of what could potentially become a healing path for many, but most especially, for *me*. I learned that when you try to heal the world, you have got to start with yourself. This was the premise behind my decision to write this book. It became my kuleana.

In the mix of doing all my personal development work, Dr. John Demartini appeared in my life. I took his seminar, the "Breakthrough Experience" in Honolulu. A major point he shared stuck in my mind. He encouraged us to write our own benefit book. Later on, Dr. Demartini and I met for lunch, and he asked me a few poignant questions, the most revealing being this: Why don't you create your own legacy right now? This combined with life at home when my ex-husband gave me a check for more than the monthly amount deemed by the court, led to an extraordinary blending of ideas that today is known as *The Benefit of the Ex: Making Love Visible When Everything Changes*.

One day, while walking along the Waikiki boardwalk, I got an idea for a television show. I could interview guests about what love meant to them and start an entirely new idea from my inner questioning. I was elated when my friend was just as excited as I was about the show's premise. She even helped me get certified with the camera and then produced a program focused on love that was all my own.

It's All About Love aired one hundred eighteen segments monthly over nine years before I chose to retire the program. Through television, I became re-enlivened about finishing my book. The story was no longer just about me, but it now included others that were working in their lives to make love visible as well.

The book had gone through several stages. I worked with a colleague who helped gather my thoughts, then I worked with my editing and writing coach, Patrick Snow, who helped me revise my manuscript. After thirteen years of work and fifty-plus stories shared by people around the globe, I took a break.

FINDING MY KULEANA

After my marriage, my personal life grew into a mess. Writing about it didn't seem to help. I craved a way to clean it up somehow, so I did what we all do when we are in times of trouble: I called my mom. My mother, Margie, gave me some free advice: "If you are stuck, then the only way to fix your life is to volunteer. You need to go be of service."

She told me that the only way to heal was to get out of my own way and help others. I explained to her about all my work in the community, volunteering at the women's prison, facilitating Toastmasters, and starting a public television show called *It's All About Love*. My mother still felt like it wasn't enough. "Do more," she urged.

The following Sunday while sitting in Unity Church of Hawaii, they announced that the church was looking for people to be of service in the men's prison system. I decided to join the three other women who went into two prisons twice a week and offer what I could to help. Simultaneously, I attended *A Course in Miracles* twice a week and was enrolled in the Spiritual Education and Enrichment S.E.E. program with Unity. Years later, I would eventually make the decision to become a Licensed Unity Teacher, and today, I'm studying to become an ordained Unity minister.

One of the mainstays of this book is the concept of being of service. While this is the colloquial phrasing of the word, it's more conceptually correct to say being in service. When you are in service, you are actively working to serve. Whereas, the common phrasing suggests that, like me, you can somehow be about service and not actually be fully in service. This simple act of pushing myself to serve deeper, created opportunities that were entirely unforeseen by me.

For example, I met a new friend during this time who was a wedding officiant. Toni had a thriving wedding business on the island and invited me to join her. She saw that I was a natural presenter and sensed that I would be a perfect fit to conduct wedding ceremonies as an officiant. A few months later, after accepting the offer, I realized I could do it myself, but I didn't want to be in competition with my friend. So, I decided to ask Toni for her blessing to open up my *own* wedding business. Toni, responded, "There is enough love and money for everyone; how can I support *you*?"

Today, my wedding business, I Do Hawaiian Weddings, thrives at about eighty ceremonies per year, primarily from couples from all around the globe. My ceremonies include all orientations, genders, cultures, and religious backgrounds. Most days, I travel around the island feeling like I am living in a dream.

DOING SOMETHING OUT OF THE ORDINARY

Shortly after I started this new business, I attended a TED Talk mixer in Honolulu. As guests checked in, the front desk receptionist asked them to share their kuleana with her and then with everyone else. The intention was to discover what we all were doing to live accountably and with integrity. When she asked what my kuleana was, I replied automatically, "To make love visible." The receptionist was momentarily stunned and responded, "Wow, that's *cool!*"

Touched by this moment and the surprised look on my friend's face who was with me, I immediately felt a deepening sensation within myself, and I knew that it was how I wanted to spend the rest of my life feeling. It was ironic, because my friend told me many months before, "June bug, you make love visible wherever you go."

Today, *making love visible* has become my answer to how we can benefit from any former relationship, event, or trauma when we make love visible by *being love* in the world. To do this, we must first love ourselves, and then find love for each other. The expression of this mission will be explained more in-depth as we progress through this journey of love.

Invitation ~ Pen and Paper

If you haven't tried journaling, I invite you to begin now. You may have a long list of reasons (*excuses*) as to why you can't or don't want to write. I am asking that you give it a shot this time and see what comes from putting your thoughts down in ink. Be gentle with yourself. One day at a time. Soon enough you will have thirty days filled in your journal. Every once and awhile gaze into the mirror for self-reflection, for answers.

It isn't easy. You have got to sit with yourself, your thoughts, and your judgments. You have got to be patient. Be still and ask for guidance. What does asking sound like? One of the most powerful ways that we can do this is by asking ourselves this question daily: What good can come from this?

In my own journaling practice, I have found that working with positive affirmations is a great way to give myself a sense of hope. Remember that affirmations are simply a tool that can help you to adopt a brighter outlook, which can lead you closer to the truth. You may also find reverse affirmations called *denials*, supportive in letting go of attachments, worry, and doubt.

Denials are a great way to affirm change. For example, "This _____ has no power over me." Statements like this build relief and trust within ourselves that let us know we will be okay. *A Course in Miracles* by Helen Schucman and William Thetford, poses the question: "Would you rather be right or happy?" This is an excellent question to ponder when you find yourself with your need to be right getting in the way of your true happiness.

The more you read and think about the topics, the more you will add to your journal. If you started a daily journal, feel free to go ahead and add to it and keep everything in one place. If you bring your ideas, thoughts, intentions, and feelings into your reading, you will grow from this work.

The goal of creating your journal is to have a personal resource that helps you to catalogue the feelings and revelations that you become aware of as you continue to expand your concept of what love is and where the benefits in your past relationship are.

Journaling Steps:

Use the following as guidelines. Keep in mind you can write whatever comes to mind, but if you are stuck, feel free to revert to this list to gain ideas or enhanced clarity on what kinds of entries will help you the most.

Grab a blank book and a pen, find a quiet space, and begin reflecting. Remember, ask yourself concrete questions: "Why am I angry?" Or "What can I do to improve my love life?" Write down any feelings of gratitude you have about your new life, even minor things, such as a new pet or weight loss, are appropriate. More emotional aspects, such as renewed freedom, more self-confidence, or a freer mind are appropriate as well.

- Write down your thoughts quickly so thoughts of judgement don't intervene.

- Read what you have written. How does it make you feel? Is it true? Or have you discovered that you have lied to yourself?

1. Document your growth as an individual through minor things you've noticed about yourself such as this: "Last Week, I went to a party for the first time in three years, and I felt a renewed sense of aliveness and wellbeing."

2. Chronicle any lessons you've learned or are currently learning and be sure to write the backstory to how you found yourself in this position and where you hope it leads.

3. What was one unexpected benefit that you *never* thought would come after your ex experience? How do you feel now that this benefit is in your life?

4. Be honest with yourself: How much better is your life today as a result of your ex or a former experience in your life? Are you a different person? Are you a better person? If so, how?

5. What haven't you been able to forgive or release about the other person (or experience as a whole) that is hurting you, or causing you undue emotional trauma? What aspects of yourself do you still need to forgive?

6. Where do you feel you need to grow the most? What could you do to reach out and get help or mentorship on where to go next?

7. What have friends or family recognized about you that they didn't prior to your conscious separation? (If recovering from addiction or similar issue: How have they accepted the positive changes?)

8. What would you like to see change in your mood, attitude, or mindset that you can start working on today and build on in the coming weeks and months? What can you do to proactively help get yourself to that point?

Remember, these are just some ideas to help you get the creative juices flowing. As you proceed with your reading and reflect on these ideas and concepts, please add any notes, questions, or revelations you may experience. The goal of *The Benefit of the Ex* is to awaken you to your own truth, and to allow you the experience of learning more about yourself. Filling in a benefit journal is a primary step in helping you document your own personal journey of discovery.

CHAPTER 2

Traversing Our Landscape

"Your task is not to seek for love, but merely to seek and find all the barriers within yourself that you have built against it." - Rumi

The ex in our lives is valuable because the pain of our memories makes way for a dynamic force that moves us forward to getting what we say we really want. A failed relationship shows us what we don't want, versus what we do want. It is the direct opposite of what we desire. Failure and our inability to get what we want can cause us to hide for fear of judgment. Or, it can be a stabilizing force that gives us perspective on what we really need in our lives. Without setbacks, divorce, or change, we wouldn't grow and have the ability to live our lives to the fullest. Change is part of living and how you handle the change is how we learn to make better decisions the next time.

FAILURE LEADS TO CHANGE

Our history books are filled with people who thought that the only door open to them in life was slammed shut, but when another door opened, they created a life that they loved despite their earlier failures. We wouldn't have the light bulb if it weren't for the ten thousand times Thomas Edison failed. Michael Jordan said, "I've missed more than nine thousand shots in my career. I've lost almost three hundred games. Twenty-six times I've been trusted to take the game winning shot and missed. I've failed over and over and over again in my life. And that is why I succeed."

Similarly, a newspaper editor fired Walt Disney because "he lacked imagination and had no good ideas." He went bankrupt several times before he built

Disneyland. In fact, the proposed park was rejected by the city of Anaheim on the grounds that it would only attract riffraff.

Even the first time Jerry Seinfeld walked on stage at a comedy club as a professional comic, he looked out at the audience, froze, and forgot the English language. He stumbled through ninety seconds of material and was jeered offstage. He returned the following night and closed his set to wild applause. The point is that these are just stories and I share them as examples of what's possible for you. They also offer another way to look at living a life of love.

Too many people have had exes that have resulted in stunted growth. Why? It's not because someone rejected you, or because you've become debilitated due to a disease, or had a chapter in your life close. The reason that setbacks can stunt your forward momentum is because they invoke doubt, fear, and suspicion that new growth is possible. And more importantly, when you aren't willing to look at growing, you will remain stuck until you are ready to finally change. Or, you can be stuck on repeat—doing the same thing over and over again, expecting your results to change.

It's no secret that we have a merit-based society. It is one that calls upon us to seek out accomplishment and bases our rewards on our performances. We get rewarded for good works and punished for what is deemed inappropriate or lackluster. Being faced with our own weakness can be challenging. The questions we need to ask are how do they change us and why?

Our expectations are to blame and account for why failure changes us. When our expectations are not met, we tend to have an experience of disappointment in some form or another. If we are willing to let go of expectation and let the Universe correspond with the nature of our song or asking, a greater success has room to occur. We can't cope with the mismatch between what we expected and our reality. Feeling like we've encountered a setback can potentially happen any time that we have an expectation. Expectations stem from our projected beliefs about what will happen in the future and how our past laid the groundwork for formulating ideals that we now hold as unchangeable truths. While expecting great things is one of the tenants of being able to realize your dreams, it is also a way to deceive yourself into never actually feeling the gift of your present moment. We are trained in our society to feel like the process of any sort of ex is a pronouncement of failure. We've become such perfectionists! We expect things to go right the first time, even when we know that there's a lot of work to be done and that growing is part of achieving mastery in anything we want to accomplish. Failing is an experience that seems to force us to shut down and close ourselves off to new opportunities. Usually, fear of failure is debilitating unless we are willing to see it as an invitation to change or a transition from the old to something new.

When we close ourselves off, we close off something that is absolutely vital to our lives running smoothly: an open heart where possibilities are endless.

When we push forward to get through our lives, it results in the continuation of beating ourselves up for fear that things won't go better next time around, or worse yet—that whatever we have created will never change.

It is rare that anything positive comes from you spending a night with the only two men in your life: Ben and Jerry. Crying, watching movies, and diving head-first into the ice cream bowl isn't going to get you any closer to where you want to be. In fact, it may only make matters worse!

We shortchange ourselves because of our inability to live our lives after something bad has happened to us. Our minds tell us that the same thing that happened before will repeat itself, and so we freak out. What's worse, we hold these thoughts in our minds so that they keep reproducing. Ultimately, we find it harder to trust in the openness that led us to where we said we wanted to be.

Maybe you wanted to marry your partner and your partner decided that it wasn't meant to be. Or perhaps you are so used to getting rejected in your life that you punish yourself for being wrong. The truth is, you are actually only failing at one thing: realizing that your mistakes always lead you closer to making the right decisions.

We change after an expectation has been broken, either with ourselves or with others. We change because we make judgments on how we think something should be. When there is disagreement, two things can happen: we hold onto a grudge and remain miserable, or we let go and move on.

Life isn't as *linear* as it seems. We treat life like it's a series of pre-planned goals and objectives, which is admittedly part of the makeup of our lives. Yet, there is so much more to the story. Life, like the ocean, has its own rhythms, and we each must learn to adjust our sails to chart our own course. Some mornings we wake up and the toilet doesn't want to flush or the dog threw up on the rug. Or maybe your flight is delayed, which shifts your travel plans. You can plan all you want; life will still put obstacles in your way. It is how you choose to navigate them that makes the difference.

THE STAGE

In our current smartphone device-driven era, we've become so connected to our peers that we are paradoxically cut off from them. We think that sending a casual message may be too invasive, and sometimes we fail to ever follow up at all because we aren't *truly connected*. What happened to simply calling?

We've become increasingly riddled with fears of future failures, and our minds begin to play endless loops about what could possibly go wrong. Yet, it doesn't have to be that way. This is a tough point but remember, *no one is making you do anything*. It's always up to you to choose. Is your cup half full or half empty? Check in with your thinking and look for the good that is really present.

We've exchanged our carefree world of childhood daydreaming for a life that is much smaller than what we intended. We don't set aside personal time nor partnership time because something has got to get done first. We will never get it done! Our thoughts are inundated with goals that must have tangible outcomes. We are missing out on the intrinsic delights of introspection and self-reflection. Breaking yourself free from your *ex* is important because it is what opens you up to the joy of playing once again. It supports you in carrying out your vision of a fulfilled life. But playing is more of a process than a fixed system of rules. It's not something that you can consciously *plan on doing*. Instead, you have got to consciously *and consistently* plan on playing by letting your mind invite in the thought "what would this feel like" and choosing your next step.

Playing is a way of being—just like being angry, sad, or frustrated is a way of being. The former shows up when you are feeling great about life, and the latter finds you when stress has you captive. To turn this around, you need to create momentum with change. When you figure out how to become captivated again, you can reactivate your natural sense of joy and wonder. When this occurs, all sorts of changes will happen. You will feel alive and become determined enough to keep trying it until you begin to lighten up. Can you be captivated again? What would reactivate your natural sense of wonder? It could be creating a vision board for all your dreams to be up on your wall or taking a trip to somewhere you imagined since you were little. Lighten up, relax, and let the changes flow through you as you become the unfoldment of love in motion.

Having the courage to feel a sense of awe and wonder isn't difficult. Likewise, creating momentum enough to change your attitude isn't hard. But there are a couple of guidelines that might influence you towards fixing a bad attitude.

PAIN CAN CAUSE GROWTH

While play encourages us to live outside of the box, pain is a useful tool for learning on many dimensions. I call pain a *tool for transformation*. Through pain and joy, I learned that *making love visible* becomes a way to breathe life into what our life's work is really all about. When you live in the possibility of what can happen, instead of the fear of what might happen, it becomes a way for you to make the best of yourself known. It takes noticing the subtle changes going on underneath the surface within yourself.

Ask yourself if you are keeping yourself stuck, or can you let go of the thought and move into the possibility of what could be next. Living is not always easy to do. When you are stuck in a place of scarcity or feel overwhelmed, nothing seems possible. Every unique situation, no matter how bad the wreckage, can become your beautiful masterpiece, if you are willing to see it.

Your greatness may be wrapped up in the past, or in a former lover, marriage, or a relationship of significance to you. The part of you that was compelled to pick up this book, wants to find out what lies ahead in life, and the hopeful possibility of what new greatness awaits. When you begin to discover that letting your own light shine is what you are here for, others around you begin to light up too.

You Have A Responsibility

On your way to learning more about who you are, you have to recognize something: Every human being has an opportunity to make love visible in his or her own life and in the lives of others. This means getting past what holds us back. This is a bold statement and yet, what are we really here for? Every human being is a dynamic individual. Most people are so over-involved, they never take the time to get to know themselves. This epidemic runs so deep in our society and is inherent in everything we do, it has become who we are. From the busy lives we lead, to the jobs that occupy much of our time, life gets in the way of us living it to the fullest. In fact, we run away to live! Vacations, holidays, nights at the bar, and even hours spent on social media take us away from our problems, only to return us to our doorstep where we have to eventually deal with our pain.

Our cultural filters set us up for the desire to marry, have children, take on activities with family and friends, and live a certain standard that we think is right. Then we discover it's not what we really wanted, or thought that it was, and see that our choices no longer serve us as individuals. To dive deeper into what it means to serve ourselves, we have got to understand what we need. This means asking the hard questions of what's underneath the ideas you are holding for yourself and perhaps for others, then looking even deeper as to what is underneath those beliefs. Loving yourself is a process. It isn't taught to us in school, at home, in church, or in college. Loving our self is something that we *all* struggle with, and something that takes re-learning on a daily basis. Actually, feeling the peace of self-love is the ultimate freedom, because it frees us from the mind-bending thoughts of a break-up from the past, from the fear of the future, and from the insecurities that get in the way of living in the present moment. It is a journey and one of our many life lessons we must learn, and usually, the experience occurs when we least expect it. Those are the gifts that become abundant with prosperity for our future to grow upon.

Learning how to love ourselves is a journey of respect on all levels. Having respect for someone is an implied agreement in any type of relationship. So, it makes sense that having love for ourselves starts with learning how to respect our own wishes, our own desires, and our own inner journey of awareness. The more self-aware we become, the easier it is to find new reasons for respecting ourselves.

Respect is the foundation of honor, and honor is the cornerstone of integrity, humility, and trust. As my stepfather Bob once said, "You are only as good as your word. It's all you've got." When you begin to recognize your truth through your word, integrity becomes a foundational building block for your life. The journey of self-discovery and learning to live by your word begins when you learn to trust yourself just as fully as the process that you are creating. This happens when you are willing to be honest with both yourself and with those that touch your life.

Trusting yourself is something that you can only appreciate by growing into it. Falling in love instantly is a rarity because love builds up over time and hits critical mass. "Falling in love" is an entirely different topic and yet part of the same internal journey. It is the journey to get to that point that makes us whole. And it is a journey of momentum.

Imagine what your life might be like if you fell in love with *yourself*? Does that question make you uncomfortable? I noticed that when I first asked myself that, all sorts of uncomfortable feelings popped up. If we are ever to uncover what it is that we honestly want in our lives, we must learn to accept situations, to respect ourselves, trust ourselves, and finally to say, "Yes, I love me!" This isn't easy, but it's definitely doable!

WHO SHOULD WE BLAME?

To work with the intention of trusting and respecting ourselves, it is paramount that we do a little "light blaming." Blame can be useful, just as justifiable anger can be useful, to help alleviate repressed negative emotions we are harboring toward ourselves. However, it is important that we learn to recognize and grow to accept that other people are not to be blamed for where we are in our lives. Choices have been made by all parties, and while the outcome may hurt now, they are all for the highest good.

Certainly, there have been instances where you have felt wronged, hurt, ruined, or rejected. Resentment will build if you do not learn to release your negativity toward other people as well as yourself. By resisting, you will stay exactly where you are. Resistance has the potential to turn into resentment and revenge if it is not addressed in the beginning. The need to be right is the most damaging path because it often leads to more conflict.

One of the toughest things I had to realize on my journey was that my divorce wasn't all my partner's fault. He wasn't to blame for the pain or for the unhappiness I was feeling. I wanted to believe he was. I wanted to be right about his actions rather than speaking into what "I" couldn't live with any longer. On rare occasions, I still have heartache, but it has also been an incredibly contemplative and rich journey. Upon reflection, I am grateful for the years that I spent with Ray because they provided a foundation for my future to grow.

The key question you must ask yourself is this: Am I willing to accept that *some of it* was my fault and I made choices that got me where I currently am? Because after all, we've made many of the choices. Bear in mind, our *need to be right* can get in the way of *our need to heal*.

That little question, "Am I willing to accept that some of it was my fault?" acts like a sticky note pinned to the front of your forehead; every time you want to cry, scream, or call a friend to vent, remember that it is there looking back at you in the mirror. The truth is we have no idea who we are. We know deep down what it is like to be authentic, but we are also overly concerned with what others think of us. This is what I like to call the "looking good" program. It runs in the background of our mind as a safety mechanism and gets triggered when we are afraid to be vulnerable. We will do anything we can to avoid looking inward; seeing ourselves for who we are can be a nightmare!

This journey is about stepping out of the shadows and into the limelight of your heart so that your actions echo your soul's calling. To take ownership of who you are, you have to realize that you can't consciously give yourself to someone one hundred percent until you have given one hundred percent to yourself. There will always be a piece of you that is neglected if you don't pay attention to *you* first.

A relationship, whether it is with a partner, a church, a friend, a pet, a hobby, or an addiction, cannot require everything from you. It can only take a piece, and it can only take what you allow it to. That is the secret to relationships: A relationship is only as strong as the magic you put into it.

The next step is learning to celebrate the glory of who you are as you learn to make love visible in your own life, and then open up to share that newfound love in the lives of others. The only person you owe a commitment to is to yourself. When you have this realization and begin to work it into your life, it is only then that you will begin to be prepared to bring someone else in. Have you ever heard the phrase, "it takes one to know one," "like attracts like," or "they are a mirror reflection of you?" It's not the easiest thought to swallow because we typically see what we don't like about someone and possibly it is because we recognize something in them that we have ourselves. This is especially true when we notice something in someone else that we don't like. It is often our own actions that need to be explored, not the other person's. Other people, just like life circumstances, can have an odd way of mirroring back to us what we want to ignore. When we begin to grow in our own inner honesty, the invitation to look at ourselves becomes clear. The question is when do you want to begin? This invitation to look at ourselves is perhaps the richest magic in this book, simply because it is so often forgotten in our culture.

Our lives are a celebration of our struggles, triumphs, and collaborations. Marriage, partnerships, and a variety of relationships are all something that honors us—not just the other party. When you begin to release your pain and recognize a loss in your life, you see that the work that you are doing is supportive. This means that you are on your way to something new that's just for you. You are accepting the invitation!

We romanticize relationships between couples, but we don't have any way of romanticizing the feelings we have for ourselves. Wouldn't it be wonderful to feel it was actually "alright" to fall in love with yourself and to not be judged, or to be called conceited or self-centered? What would this even feel like?

WHAT DOES LOVE MEAN?

One of the biggest questions that I had to ask myself before I could fall in love with myself was, "What does love even mean?" It was fundamental to my growth and spiritual maturity in understanding how to show up as a loving person in the world in order to make my *kuleana* visible to others. It was no longer enough to sit and sulk or to wait to be rescued. If love was real, then I wanted to find out for myself what it really was, and how I could use it to bring out the best in myself and in others.

Love is one of those all-encompassing words that means just about everything these days. Paradoxically, it has also been watered down in our text message era to mean almost nothing. On one hand, we are struck by the fear of saying those three little words to our romantic partners because it changes the intensity of the relationship. And while, in one instance, we are afraid to be vulnerable, popular conversation includes off-handed remarks such as "Oh, I love her dress," or "I love that idea!" In this way, we fall short of being able to ascribe any actual meaning to the word when it becomes lost in a material world of quick expression and vernacular turn of phrase.

This chapter isn't about picking apart whether or not emojis are ruining our communication, or what we mean when we tell our child "I love you." It's about understanding Love's variety, which leads us ever closer to discovering Love's depths.

These are merely the semantics behind a word that many would argue rules so much of our lives. This is because whether we realize it or not, we are all seeking love in various ways. We seek one or both ends of the spectrum—either to give love, to receive love, or both.

It's true that *Love* is one of the most difficult words in the English language to explain—let alone to deconstruct to understand the written form. Some people wrestle with it, much like every attempt by famous philosophers throughout history, while others seek to make a concerted effort to ignore it. In truth, the context of love goes far beyond just learning to love a committed partner, job, or child. To me, Love extends to the furthest corners of our beings. When you start to delve deeper into the inner workings of the heart, mind, and spirit, you learn that the spectrum of love is broader than most of us ever knew was possible.

LOVE FOR OURSELVES, LOVE FOR OTHERS, AND EMPATHY

Consider the feelings you have when you watch a sad movie. Why do we cry? If we *know* that the characters aren't real, then why do they seem so believable? This is because as humans we exhibit empathy and compassion.

Compassion springs from the sensitivity that exists within all of us. As separate individuals, we are challenged with the ability to embrace others, just as we must embrace ourselves. Having compassion is about being sensitive to the warmth and love that exists within our inner journey. When we awaken and listen to what our hearts are truly telling us, we can pick up on the need for movement, growth, and change. It is the mediator that steps in between two fighting children on the playground and wants growth. It is the parent or partner who is open to discussion before getting flustered. No matter what happens, when we witness the existential nature of the human condition—at any level—it is difficult to take in and understand. Abject poverty anywhere, for example, can be gut-wrenching to observe. We may not know this experience first-hand, but we have all lived through something that was challenging. These feelings drive us to connect deeper with other human beings to share our struggles. However, when we ourselves go through a rock-bottom experience, we find it difficult to give ourselves the acceptance and self-love that we deserve. Permission is at the root of this understanding, and it is in permission that we learn to love ourselves completely. We must permit ourselves to be who we are.

One of our biggest struggles as a human being is dealing with the concept of how we can love others and offer them a compassionate response with ease, even when being faced with our own challenges. It's hard to be helpful in times of pain. There are two extremes to this type of difficulty. The first is the isolator or the hermit that seals themselves off from society doing nothing to heal themselves. While this may be worthwhile, divine, and necessary in certain situations, it can become an unfortunate habit in other scenarios. Cutting yourself off from people is not a productive way to deal with pain. Unfortunately, many don't recognize when they do this, but it is something that we all must learn to break if we want love to be an active reality in our lives.

The second extreme is just as bad but appears to be better on the surface. People in the opposite extreme focus so much time on others that they ignore their own needs. Instead, we must search for a balance between our needs and the needs of others. Throughout our life, there are times that call for isolation, reflection, and meditation and there are also times that call for charity, community, and joining together.

LOVE IS ALL THE RAGE

Love wants to be shared. Love wants to be expressed. Love wants to be spread around to all who can partake in its grandness. And Love wants to be Love. Meaning, that it wants to show up in the world and claim its own greatness.

Love is reciprocation and an invitation *simultaneously*. It is a spectrum, which desires to be both giving and receiving. On one end of the spectrum, you must give love to have it. Giving love means you must be able to sink your entire spirit into it and squeeze it into the depths of your being. And on the other end of the spectrum, are Love's open hands extended for you to grab onto whenever you need support. This is the beauty of what love's spectrum can represent in our lives.

Invitation ~ Script the Benefits

One of the most expedient ways to clear up your negative thinking behind whatever has happened is to write the benefits of your former relationship. *A what?* Script the Benefits means to document the benefits of your ex. This is one of the greatest ways to consciously shift your awareness of what has happened, what is happening, and what you want to create in the future. If you want a different future, you need to adopt different beliefs about what happened and what you are creating to be able to change.

Everyone who risked writing his or her story for this book said thank you afterwards. It was an unintended consequence of putting themselves out there. They had no idea what would come of being willing to lay it down and actually look at the benefits of their former relationship.

A script of benefits is a remedy that can help you to become more aware of what you believe, what you would rather believe instead, and how you can make the switch to believing more of what you want to believe. This documentation is a reflective process.

So how do you create a Script of Benefits? By writing down: (1) your wins, (2) what you have created, (3) what habits you've let go of, (4) new discoveries about anything that you are free of, and (5) how your life is affected. Maybe it's seeing a softness in your eyes and how it feels to be in a new realm of personal understanding or what it's like to live alone and not have to have the toilet paper a certain way! Here we consider how to build momentum in the opposite direction towards forgiveness, compassion, and understanding. The more we work in that direction, the easier it will be to move forward in our own lives. The goal isn't to jot everything down right now. Instead, as you read through this book, hopefully you will have insights that inspire you to write more. In other words, this is an ongoing process that should continue long after you are done with the pages of this book.

CHAPTER 3

Desiring Love's Spectrum

Never make someone a priority when all you are
to them is an option." - Maya Angelou

What is the heart of the problem? Our universal fear of accepting Love. When we learn about why we must face our fear and the unconscious associations that cause us to fall short of our full potential, we can open ourselves up to explore the bravery we all know exists inside of us. This bravery is an acquired strength. The more you practice it, the better you will be at acting on your own highest interest towards what your heart desires most. Seeking Love through desire requires us to open up our hearts and learn how to truly love ourselves.

WE SEEK LOVE FOR CLARIFICATION

We look for Love everywhere. We search for it when we choose a college, a new car, or pick out a new partner. We want to feel like we are being supported and that we are correct in our assumptions. We seek Love and understanding from our spouses when we decide to discipline our children. We look for others to give us a metaphorical "pat-on-the-back" after we select a profession and succeed or obey our parents' wishes for our lives.

Somewhere in the middle of this spectrum, we seek validation for our choices. We want to give Love, but we are afraid that we will be laughed at, mocked, or rejected ourselves. We want someone to call us and tell us we are on the right track.

THE HEART OF THE PROBLEM

To reach Love, we must face our inner tiger with courage and be willing to participate in the unknown. It takes faith that must be placed in ourselves, first.

Having faith doesn't exclusively mean having faith in *God*, or any one religious idea. It just means that you believe that what you are doing in life can work itself out, and no matter how small, you are able to see evidence of that truth becoming evident in your life.

The truth is that you can feel infinite, joyous, and free right now. You are free to change your mind at any time and feel differently about your life's circumstances and your reality. You don't need anyone's permission either.

You may never need to read another self-help book or seek out counsel. You can heal yourself by *remembering to love yourself*. The truth is that most people would rather be rescued, rather than discover the secret to their own healing, because that takes work. We want to be guided, coaxed, and gently nudged out of our shells.

Leaving a familiar and comfortable place feels as if you are about to jump out of a moving airplane. It feels scary and it can provoke fear and anxiety. It also causes us to want to retreat to our comfortable environment, even though that can be even more unhealthy for us. When we decide to say *yes*, it becomes a tool for our own inner expansion and transformation. Saying *yes* can be frightening at times, but commitment becomes the fuel that propels us forward. Discovering your still, small voice in action gives you suggestions, guidance, and perspectives to help you open the door to your heart, and to let yourself feel the love of your own unique expression.

TREKKING FEAR MOUNTAIN

If you have ever climbed up a mountain, you have to start at the foot of the mountain where you begin the ascent. It's the only way. It can be difficult, and it is much easier when you are ready to move and begin the climb. If you've never taken on something that seems insurmountable (and I'm not saying Mt. Everest), you find it takes time and courage. It is the same as you to begin the act of examining the benefits of your ex. Your view will be changed forever. Once you reach the top, your perspective will be different.

WHY WE DON'T CLIMB THE MOUNTAIN

Just beyond the mountain of our fear is a shadow. This is the mist that hides what lies on the other side. In Hawaii, we sometimes experience *"vog,"* and no, this is not a typo. I can assure you; volcanic fog is actually a thing and it filtrates through the air of the island whenever the trade winds are blowing just right.

Vog: n. *smog or haze containing volcanic dust and gases.*

Example in a sentence: *There was a layer of vog hanging over our side of the island this morning.*

Volcanic islands are formed by volcanic activity on the seabed, often near the boundaries of the tectonic plates that form Earth's crust. Where two plates pull apart, lava erupts to form an undersea ridge. Layers of lava build up until a ridge breaks the sea's surface to form an island.

Without a volcanic eruption, Hawaiians wouldn't be living on the land that they so gracefully inhabit today. It's perfect that a natural disaster gave birth to the beauty that we now know as the archipelago chain of islands called the Hawaiian Islands. Could this be what you are going through? *Remember, you are the "I" of the storm.* What this means is that the more your ability to see safely to the center of the storm is obscured, the scarier the journey feels.

When we seek Love, it takes action to find it. Some of these actions will be joyful, like seeing a beautiful view from the top of a peak. While, some will be painful, like having to climb up a steep mountainside when it is slick with fresh rain. Putting in the work required to make the most of your life is important. Avoidance can be easy. Asking yourself *"what would Love do?"* may change your life forever. It forces us to find the inner courage to commit to action.

GETTING AROUND FEAR

You are the captain of your own fate, and setting sail is all part of the job description. Bridging the gap between what you want and what you have to do to get there can be a little scary. Like walking on a rickety wooden bridge in the Hawaiian jungle for instance. If we fall, others may see. And if we get across, they may think we are crazy for trying something so ridiculous. However, getting over the mountain is simply a metaphor for getting over your fear.

WHAT IS DESIRE?

When we get past our fear, we begin to want more out of our life. Fear keeps us stuck. It forces us to play safe. It suggests that maybe we aren't all we thought we would be. Maybe our self-doubts were right. When we escape the "ex" that fear creates in our lives, we begin to seek out newness. Like being released from a prison, we begin to want to create and expand. This requires courage. With this courage, we begin to *desire* the best possible future for ourselves. In our culture, desire is quickly misunderstood. So, what is desire, really?

Desire is what moves us to take action, to think the thoughts that we choose, and to make decisions. Desire is not the journey itself. Desire is the forethought that fuels and propels the journey; it is the appetizer that whets your appetite and gets you ready for more. While this desire is divinely designed in us, desire gets a bad rap within our popular culture. We are taught not to desire lustfully, or to be *unrealistic*. Instead, we decide to settle into what we feel is a safe life, and we create an even safer identity for ourselves. When in reality, we need to be brave and follow our desires to see the truth of where they lead.

In Western society, we need to remember that desire is not the enemy. It can actually be our best friend taking us to places that we didn't expect, in addition to doing things that we never imagined we would do. Desire is an *opening*. It's a statement to the Universe that says, *"Hey, I want that!"*

After you desire something, *acknowledge* it exists. This creates the decision and the spark to move forward and grow. It is both emotional and physical.

The purpose of desire is expansion. When we desire an ice-cream cone or a cup of coffee, we deliberately decide that ice cream or espresso is *exactly* what we need in that moment. That is the trajectory of our path—at least for the moment. In taking that action, we create something that is definitive, if not ideal for us.

Desire isn't just about creating waves in the Universe for momentary pleasure. Desire also enables the chambers of our heart to flood open. By consciously saying "yes" to desire, it gets us into a type of flow, or surrendering to the expansion that can now occur. Whenever we expand, it creates momentum towards bringing us more of what we want. This is the truest purpose of desire—to enable us towards seeking and finding a greater realization of ourselves. When we begin to find new aspects of ourselves, we begin the process of growth. Growing is painful at times, but it is always a worthwhile experience that leads you into a greater feeling of wholeness. It is a little strange to think about, but desire leads us both towards and away from our center. Let us dive a little deeper into what that entails.

DESIRING ANYTHING MEANS YOU'RE
CURRENTLY LACKING SOMETHING

Desire leads us towards expansion and towards greater wholeness. However, in stating that we desire something, there's also an inherent lack associated with it. In addition, when desire turns into anger, bitterness, or resentment, it separates us from being centered in our self. Either scenario keeps us from being present and missing the gifts that may lay right before us.

While desire encapsulates the concept of "not having something presently," it is also a great exercise in expansion (hence the paradox). At the same time, desire is healthy, acceptable, and can lead to the vibrant fulfillment of who you are. Making love visible is *only* possible through desire. Without the appetite for making Love palpable in the world—there is no way to actually make Love visible. Visibility craves to be seen, and desire is what gives us the willingness to follow through on our intentions. Desire is the finger that pushes our buttons! In other words, desire is what gets us going, lights us up, motivates us and inspires us toward new experiences.

DESIRE IS GOOD

So hopefully, we've dispelled some of your thoughts about desire. Desire in its purest form is unadulterated intention. Many spiritual people, doctors, politicians, and pastors desire to serve humanity, which takes us deeper than desire and into the territory of Love. Serving humanity while serving oneself is the single greatest gift of self-discovery.

Desire is also complex. When you are moving through a myriad of desires and life situations, your desires need to be clear. Otherwise, the Universe has no idea how to correspond with your wishes. By maintaining feelings of uncertainty, you risk drifting into any random situation that comes along.

For example, if you've ever been to a new car lot, guitar store, or dress shop—and you just can't decide because the choices are so overwhelming—then you know what I'm referencing. This is a time where you can be swept up in the joy of decision-making, go wild and buy one of each, or simply leave with nothing, wondering what just happened. The choice, whichever choice you choose, is always yours.

The difficulty, and the complexity, is in being judicious in knowing what your heart truly desires. Sometimes, it's simply waiting. The space in between the answers can often provide the answers.

Are you really excited for vacation or are you sick of going to the same place year after year? Desire is funny and it can be fickle. This is another reason why being grounded in your own inner sanctuary can help you make the most of your decision-making. How do you get clear on your desires? Dream big.

When you decide to desire Love, let go of the fear that wants to keep you stuck doing the same things you have always done. When you decide that you are safe living in the questions of your life and that your dreams and desires are worth it, begin to unlock faculties of your inward experience that have been waiting for you to discover more of who you really are.

The real magic of desire is when you can definitively claim what is yours—even before you have it. When one pathway closes—there are a million others that you could choose to explore. The important part is that you desire to do so. This is when you begin to discover the greatness of who you are, and how you can start making Love visible within your own spirit. You become alive in the most unexpected and delightful ways. First, in your thoughts and private meditations, then as an active part of your community and beyond.

In these moments of awakening, you will find yourself letting go of old patterns that no longer serve you and saying "thank you" to the new ones that have come forward. Gratitude for little things will find their way into your daily conversation, and your body, mind, and spirit will begin to feel open to new possibilities. The experiences of your past will become the stepping-stone for your success both now and as you traverse through your future.

At some point, you need to ask of your desires, "Is this what I really want?" It is your choice to begin whenever you are ready. You can continue to be right, or self-righteous about where you are, or you can get to work on being happy. It's all up to you. Today is for getting clear on what you want!

Desire is the great opener of possibilities, magical circumstances, amazing synchronicities and divine timing. For big things to occur in your life, you have got to be able to make room for them to develop, nourish, and grow. After all, what good is a new car if you have nowhere to store it or no place to drive it? In other words, knowing what you want and why you want it is important, but it is also necessary to be practical about making space for these things to come in and serve you in the best way possible.

I wanted to travel. I watched, observed, listened, and admired people who traveled. I drooled over their photos and hung onto the words when they posted or blogged about their amazing trips. I wanted that feeling of a carefree walk over the St. Charles Bridge in Prague. The feeling—clutching it as if it were real—is what led me to start living out this dream. It wasn't just a thought; it was a strong desire that permeated my body. I knew in my heart that it would happen, and it became a reality.

I fine-tuned my desire, and suddenly realized the barriers I built up toward traveling were gone. I had been relying on excuses: a particular friend needed to go with me, I needed to have more money in the bank, I needed to wait for retirement, or I needed to wait for when my son was old enough to move out. My excuses suddenly fell away as I imagined what it would feel like to be in Prague. I wanted to feel what I saw on the faces of those who traveled. I wanted to experience what I'd read in travel blogs, stories that were alive with enchanting discoveries of places to see and things to eat and do. My deep desire to have this experience led me to Prague in just this fashion.

The first story at the conclusion of this chapter explains how after ending his career in the military, a retired naval officer (the narrator) was able to take an honest account of his life. Hidden within his desires were unmet expectations, letdowns, and ultimately a lack of self-respect that held him back from the type of relationship he was dreaming of. He quickly realized that his past failed relationships weren't due to the way he was treated but stemmed from the much deeper, hidden feelings he held for himself. In recognizing this truth, he was able to reexamine his own thoughts and beliefs and let go of the negative self-image that had held him back. When he let go of his old self, his perfect mate arrived in made-for-Hollywood fashion and he finally got what he wanted all his life!

THIRD TIME'S A CHARM FOR A RETIRED NAVAL OFFICER: STORY ONE

"Third time's a charm!" How many times have I heard this statement from friends and family only to find out that it did not necessarily work pertaining to my own relationships? In my eyes, this statement is normally said under a veil of luck, and I now realize it was not luck that enabled me to create the relationship I am now living and actively participating in. So, for the record, I am married for the third time—and yes—this relationship is unlike any I have ever experienced before. If it is not luck, then what is it about this relationship that is different?

I have experienced numerous relationships and two successful divorces up to this point in my forty-eight years. I experienced the highs and the dull lows of being in two marriages with women whom I convincingly blamed for my eventual divorces and ensuing personal bout with depression and counseling. I entered my first marriage with mixed feelings at age twenty-four. I distinctly remember the feeling of being too young. However, I was afraid of backing out of the inevitable trajectory of where the relationship was going. I distinctly remember that my gut was telling me that I should take a better look at what I was doing. I didn't! I failed to take active control of where I was headed. Essentially, it was as though I climbed in a taxi without knowing my destination and telling the driver to drive wherever she pleased. My entire role in the relationship was passive. I did not know where I wanted to go. After five years, I exited my first marriage feeling controlled, abused, and feeling as though I was less than. I attended various personal and family counseling sessions, however, to no avail. At one point, I even experienced the embarrassment of the local police witnessing an altercation between us in public. Thankfully, the police merely spoke to both of us asking me whether I wanted to press charges. I declined. Relationships with women I dated after this marriage also seemed to flourish at first, and then after the initial period, the same personal feelings began to flare up. I was unconsciously acting out a vicious cycle of my jealousy, feeling controlled, and then being ignored. This pattern seemed to appear over and over again.

Ten years after my first marriage, I was attracted to a woman who very much fit the same physical build, personality, and familial background as my first wife. At thirty-four, I began a relationship with her, and ultimately, we chose to marry. Even though I experienced the same gut feeling, and even felt the same sensation of red flags waving in front of my face, warning me that I was making a mistake, I still chose to continue with my decision to remarry. The initial euphoria of being in a relationship with a successful professional woman who had children was amazing. For what seemed like a fleeting moment in time, I felt like I had matured because I was now a married homeowner with beautiful kids. Ah, but sadly this was not to last. The red flag waving I experienced foretold the feelings I was soon to encounter once again. After a year of marriage and experiencing the distance in the bed between us grow further apart, I was asked to leave. Once again, the police entered the situation while I was at the house, and I was asked to evacuate the premises. The only difference between the first and second marriage was that I was a homeowner and stepfather of two children the second time around. Otherwise, I repeated the same story. Was I destined to live my life repeating the same unfulfilling relationship over and over again?

Fast forward to age forty-four. I had just retired from the U.S. Navy after twenty-six years of service and was invited to attend a personal development seminar. I was informed that it might assist me in shaping the kind of career I could create after my military life. Intrigued, I attended the seminar with my main focus centered on a future career. Well, during one exercise that weekend, I had a personal experience that revealed to me why I have continuously pursued the same types of relationships, and why I repeatedly got the same results. By taking stock of my beliefs and values, I discovered how I wanted to be loved by a woman. I also discovered how I wanted to love a woman unconditionally. This was a very uplifting, encouraging, and refreshing feeling that I had not experienced previously. I took action on what I discovered about myself and since then, I have continued to work on being the best that I can be. I determined why my relationships with women continually followed a similar path.

At the seminar, I began to take responsibility for my relationships that had failed in the past and I realized that the women I had been with were not bad people, as I had told my friends and family. I realized that my ex-wives were merely treating me in response to the way I acted and viewed myself. The story I created about my marriages was that I was a victim to their controlling, dominating behavior. Of course, that is what I experienced at the time, because I was unable to see it any other way. Subsequently, I chose to take time to learn more about me, and in the process, I have discovered that I am worthy and deserving of an amazing marriage with an amazing woman.

I took the time to view all the relationships I have had with women. My relationships with my ex-wives have proven invaluable in determining what kind of marriage I want to create. I am now very grateful for the women with whom I previously blamed, had found fault, and who I had spoken about with a forked tongue. It has only been within the last four years that I have really accepted my part and taken responsibility for both my actions and the inaction that plagued my previous marriages. I realize now that I owe a debt of gratitude to both women because it is through both marriages that I learned what I really wanted.

As a result of my growth, I took action and took stock of how I wanted to feel, how I wanted to love, and how I wanted to be loved by the woman of my dreams. This is another area where I benefited from my exes. I identified areas in my past relationships that I did not like.

Armed with this knowledge, I created my extensive list of qualities and traits that I wanted in a relationship with the woman of my dreams. I focused on how I wanted to feel in this relationship. And then, it happened!

I met the woman of my dreams through a most serendipitous meeting. While waiting for a chartered bus to take me from my hotel to a seminar in Northern California, I discovered that the last bus had departed early. With no taxis available in this small town, I searched for an alternate ride. I met an old friend who was getting ready to leave the hotel also. Around the corner of his van I saw an attractive woman approach. We had briefly seen each other previously for a total of about twenty seconds, ten months earlier, but hadn't spoken. We recounted the moment we saw each other for the first time, and we described what we were wearing. It was a mutual exchange of eye contact with absolutely no words spoken. We were drawn to each other from the moment of our first glance.

Spending the entire week at the seminar in each other's company, learning about each other, we revealed that each of us had written out an extensive list of what we wanted in a relationship. And the best part was that our lists matched each other's perfectly! Surprisingly, I met thirty-eight of her thirty-nine non-negotiable items on her list, while she fit approximately ninety-five percent of mine. I attracted the woman of my dreams into my life, and together we are now creating an amazing life together. We support each other in our own goals and dreams, and we create opportunities that have never occurred to me in the past. I have become more confident in myself and in my marriage with my beautiful wife, because of our mutual respect for each other, our ability to communicate openly, and our desire to listen attentively.

I had experienced the definition of insanity by reliving the same type of relationships and expecting different results. Well, I have done something different and now I am benefiting with a new and very rewarding result: a loving, passionate, unconditional relationship with the woman of my dreams. I now view my past relationships with gratitude instead of disappointment. Because of these past experiences, I am now living a more rewarding and loving life with a woman of whom I am extremely proud. She exhibits incredible strength and courage. She raised three kids by herself, attained a vice president position without a college degree, and loves working with people. Together we are making a difference in the world.

I am no longer sitting in a taxi not knowing where I am going. My wife and I are in our own vehicle with our dreams and goals, following a roadmap of passion, fun, and fulfillment. We are truly happy together, living life to the fullest. We know that there is no limit to where we can go, what we can achieve, and how many people we can touch with unconditional love.

The couple in the story above is still together today; I even had the privilege of renewing their vows in Hawaii.

Pondering Points:

- When was a time in your life you felt lost?

- Have you ever noticed that you've ignored warning signs or weren't listening to your intuition?

In this second story, we meet an ambitious woman (the narrator) who loses everything in an attempt to have it all. Her desires are vast and taxing; she sacrifices the priority of her family to chase achievement. Her once supportive husband ends up becoming a source of her pain after he deals with his own feelings of neglect.

The Drive of an Ambitious Woman: Story Two

What is the *benefit* of my ex? The benefits begin with the knowledge that I can't expect to find something in a relationship that I haven't brought to it, which required me to take a look at how I was showing up in my past relationships. It also taught me one of the ultimate lessons in life: how to forgive. Not only did I have to forgive him for the choices he made, I had to forgive myself, too. The benefit that I received came in how I *chose* to feel about what happened.

My story begins like any other, filled with chemistry and romance and the appearance of all the right ingredients for a happy life together. Jason and I met when I was twenty years old, at a time in my life when I was absolutely sure I knew it all. I was so sure of this because I had already been married once before, knew what did and did not work in that relationship, and had a beautiful two-year-old son, Tyler.

I approached this new relationship with caution and a strong desire to make sure it was going to work before taking the plunge a second time. We dated and lived together for two years before deciding to make it official. Shortly after we were married, I applied and was accepted into the RN Program at a local university. This meant school full-time in addition to the forty hours a week I was already working to help support our new family. I knew it would be a balancing act to manage this hectic schedule, but I have always been eager to take on a challenge, and Jason had proven himself to be a great stepfather to Tyler. I knew that someday the sacrifice would be worth the temporary inconvenience.

I jumped head-first into my new roles. I committed, and I was determined to be the best I could be. Unfortunately, my school and clinical hours required a much greater commitment than I could have ever imagined. I remember waking up at 5:00 a.m. to get to school and staying up to do homework until after midnight. To be honest, most of that time in my life is a blur, like a picture out of focus. I am sure it is to protect myself from reliving something I barely made it through the first time.

To keep my sanity during this crazy time, I started running more and decided I would train to run a marathon. Again, Jason was supportive of whatever I wanted. He stepped up and took over caring for Tyler and for himself. I couldn't have made it through that time in my life without his love and support.

Life, and our relationship, started to slowly change. At the time, I was so busy *doing* that I forgot how to *be*. Time passed, and we quit spending time together. We quit communicating. We quit meeting each other's needs, and we rarely had sex. I quit bringing to the relationship what I still expected, or hoped, he would bring. I was just trying to survive, and I hoped that someday it would be better.

Two years later, with graduation one day away and a new house under construction, I could taste the victory. I had not only survived but conquered! I was graduating Phi Kappa Phi, the top 5% of my class, and was about to have my life back. What a tremendous feeling of accomplishment and relief! I couldn't believe it was finally over.

I guess that is why I never saw it coming. Finding out he had an affair was like being broadsided by something unimaginable. *It wasn't fair*. Why now, when I was so close to having my life back? Why me? What had I done to deserve this? There were so many questions, and nothing made sense. The worst part was that the affair was with someone very close to me, and she was pregnant. I remember feeling completely disoriented, like I had just been dropped in the middle of a foreign country where no one spoke my language, where I understood nothing—completely out of control. I don't remember my graduation, or if I even went.

Even though I felt betrayed, I wanted my life back. I had worked too hard to see it all fall apart now. I decided to work on forgiving him and attempted to make it work. We went to Tahiti for my graduation trip, a chance to get away and forget about the problems back home. During the trip, I found out about another affair he had with someone I had also known and trusted for a long time. That was when I lost it.

We returned home, and I filed for divorce. I turned to alcohol and more marathon training in my attempt to escape the pain. It was too much to deal with, so I just ran from my problems and hoped they would magically go away on their own. The problem is, I not only ran away from him but from everyone else I cared about. If I put enough distance between myself and everyone else, I would never have to worry about being hurt like that again. It was always there, just under the surface, waiting. I didn't face the pain of that relationship until years later, when I was married again and on the verge of my third divorce.

That was when I finally allowed it to hit me. It felt like a ton of bricks had fallen from a twenty-story building, completely crushing me. I had to allow myself to feel the pain of it all, to acknowledge that it had happened, if I ever wanted to be free. I spent countless hours devoted to personal growth to accept what had happened and the role that I had played. Through this process, I realized that I was not the victim, though I had played this role well over the past ten years. I made choices every day that defined the life I was living. Every step along the way I had a choice regarding the decisions I made, the activities I participated in, and the way I chose to live my life.

These experiences have helped define the woman I am today. I know, without a doubt, that working through the challenges I faced in our relationship helped me to embrace what it means to forgive. I will forever be grateful to him, the relationship, and the opportunity I was provided to grow!

PONDERING POINTS:

- How do you accept ownership of your past mistakes and reactions that other people have to your choices?

- How does the narrator's decision to begin running as a healthy "stress relief" turn into an isolation technique?

- What ways have you acted like our narrator?

In what ways have you sacrificed to keep a relationship healthy?

Invitation ~ Stick to Your Dreams

(For this invitation you will need **sticky notes** and a **timer**.)

Set your timer to 60 seconds. Ask yourself the following question: What does my heart desire? Once you hit the start button, write down everything on the sticky notes that you want or desire. Next, set a timer for another 60 seconds. Center yourself by taking a few deep breaths. During the next minute, gently close your eyes and empty your mind. Focus solely on your breath and the power behind your intention, what you want in life, and how you might achieve those things. Let your dreams come to life. Be aware of your own internal responses. Let your mind's chatter disappear and make room for possibilities. If you wish, take out your journal and jot down what you saw for yourself and how you felt.

CHAPTER 4

Making Room for Love

"When you are willing and eager, then gods join in." - Aeschylus

When we search for something to fill our needs, we find that almost anything feels better than nothing. This is why so many people turn to drugs, alcohol, or new relationships to fill in the empty places. However, these are only temporary fixes and aren't the kinds of whole-grain healing that nourish us.

Making room for Love is a difficult task. It calls upon us to dig deeply to the root of our *why*. This includes the good. Once we start to love the undesirable parts of who we are, by extension, we learn to love the brighter pieces we've yet to discover. This discovery is the first step towards the promise of self-love.

LOVING YOUR EXAMPLE

When you are focused on the fact that you aren't getting what you need, this creates a negative cycle. As a result, you are stuck with the same thing. If you can take a step back and remember that space is necessary for something new to come in, you can appreciate the interim as a time of preparation.

It can be uncomfortable to be single or to feel hurt when you feel someone else got the best of you. Even if your separation doesn't involve anyone close to you, it can affect much of who you are and how you are showing up in the world. The more you recognize that change can only come from planting seeds, the more you realize that seeds need time to grow. This is the in-between space where the real work gets done. When you make the decision to let go of the past and decide to set productive goals and act on them, seeds will begin to germinate.

However, the seeds of positive behaviors need nurturing as well. Nurturing ourselves is perhaps one of the most underrated skills in all Western culture. This means do you know your limits, are you getting enough sleep, are you eating well, do you have a way to relax during your day, are you taking time to get to know yourself better, are you having fun, and do you take time to feed your spiritual self? It is easy to incorporate into your everyday routine but difficult to maintain. Consistency is the key, and I'm fairly certain this isn't something you don't already know!

In our society, there is a current popular phrase called "**massive action**." This idea is based on the premise that to achieve the results you want, you must take on many tasks as quickly as possible to build momentum. Many people resonate with this because we all are, admittedly, behind on our mile-long to-do lists. To build momentum, it is important that we first focus on change.

Change opens us up to new things. Most things don't happen instantaneously. Change takes time because it takes time for us to understand the depth of our feelings.

Massive action is never the problem. Inaction is what holds us back. Slow, deliberate, consistent action is all that is really needed to make progress. Becoming *efficient* at being *consistent* is important. However, the most important revelation of overcoming our exes has got to be the common sense that we must change to get new results. While I was no longer running in the community with my ex and joining in races as a cheerleader, I found a way to fitness that lead me to new friendships. I hiked the Diamond Head Trail four to five times a week at dawn and communed with friends over coffee and scones at the nearby market's picnic tables.

We might get scared, but this fear can be used to help us learn to conquer obstacles. It can also cause intellectual or emotional paralysis. Unfortunately, no amount of advice, diet, exercise, or medication will help you to overcome fear, rather it is up to shifting your mindset; in other words, embrace fear, accept it as being a part of you but *not* you. This idea is at the core of Eastern philosophy. However, here in the West, we try to mask our fears with reckless action, which is not what massive action is about. To counter such recklessness, meditation is recommended. Creating a meditation practice can produce great results for peace of mind and prosperity, so long as it is coupled with sincere, authentic, and determined action.

Being conscious of creating space is a lot like planting a tree, to go back to our seed metaphor. Planting a tree next to a house can be aesthetically pleasing, yet the roots may eventually cause damage. Similarly, the action you thought would make everything look better may cause unforeseen damage. Sometimes, you have to uproot yourself to replant yourself in a new situation. Uprooting yourself doesn't necessarily mean moving to a new city. You can uproot your life by changing your habits, thoughts, and feelings about certain situations.

HOLDING SPACE FOR YOURSELF

At one point or another, you've probably heard the phrase "holding space" for someone. That's along the same line as saying, "I will keep him in my thoughts and prayers," or "she'll be gentle on my mind."

Holding space for someone is easy to do. It means that you will consciously be praying or actively focusing on their highest good for a set period. Maybe it's only a few minutes a day or longer. But when it comes to holding space for ourselves, sometimes we can barely remain positive for a few seconds—let alone an entire hour or more!

This is why it is vital that we learn how to make room for Love. There isn't a guidebook out there showing people how to remove pain by letting go and slowing down. Everything in our society caters to rushing into the next thing without absorbing the wisdom and warmth of what we've experienced from our past. *Want to get over a divorce? Just get a new husband or wife!*

This is not easy to grasp in its entirety because it is paradoxical. On one hand, you need to be content to deal with the gap between what you want and what is coming after the "ex." Frustration and anger can severely limit your capabilities and hold you back, which is why being happy with where you are for the moment is the key. It's also noteworthy to mention that you don't have to be content with things staying the same forever, just for the time being. To do that, what is required of you is that you open up to the possibility of what it would be like to accept your situation exactly as it is. This acceptance is what will support you in having peace.

However, to make room for that next stage, you have to be upset enough to want to change. When that happens, you can accept that what you need and what you want are no longer bookends. Instead, you can begin to open up to the idea that what you want is coming to you. Create the space, plant the seeds, be patient, and be hopeful for the future. It will grow. One of the most important decisions you can make is to be positive about the future. *Why?* Because when you are waiting for something and are happy in the interim, your quality of life is higher. You begin to forget about what you wanted, and you start to automatically accept where you are. Then, your mind begins to see other things that are going well, and your optimism has room to grow.

There is then a freshness to what you are doing and to who you are being. That fresh perspective is actually *what* you have been looking for. In many situations, *that's* really what you want, but you are calling it something else by attaching it to money, accolades, ideas of how people should act, or what they should think about you. Believe in the power of sitting and waiting with intent and optimism. If for no other reason, do so because it makes you a more productive individual during the interim.

When you can stop taking time out of your day to feel sorry for yourself, and instead can hold onto the faith with that space, you will be allowing new solutions to come to you. You will also begin to accept your current situation and your past failures as all part of a much larger plan for you.

Knowing that you can set yourself up for more love than you ever knew to ask for takes time and practice. When you do the work of understanding yourself and truly contemplating what you need to do to grow, you will be amazed at the person you become. You can even get through the pain and endless hours of struggle that it took to get there. New actions will yield new results.

When you feel angry, sad, or rejected by a situation, know that something new is coming in to replace it. Get in the habit of asking yourself, "What good can come from this?" Get a dry erase marker and write it on your bathroom mirror, the car window, or a sticky note on the refrigerator. Just put it in a place where you will see it and be reminded. It will remind you and open you up to the possibility of something good is coming your way.

Let yourself work into new ideas and allow the spirit of who you are to let go to grow. Holding on to our past experiences and complaining by telling your story over and over again is exactly what causes us to continue to feel the pain. The biggest step towards surpassing negative experiences and the fear of change is to come into presence with the here and now. Know what is actually going on around you instead of being absorbed in mentally reliving the past; this is one of the first steps to making progress. Once we get out of our heads, we create space. Remember, cultivating presence takes practice.

CREATING SPACE IN OUR MINDS

Practicing meditation is enormously important in clearing our minds and opening up our aching hearts. Indeed, there is a voice in stillness. In taking time to quiet our minds, sometimes the noisy chatter speaks to us and sometimes it's the soft whispers that guide us in letting go. As we relax, the gift of the moment emerges.

I remember when I first started to meditate. I'd start with just fifteen minutes in the morning and work my way up to thirty over time. Feeling my breath flow in and out was something I had never stopped to think about before. Noticing my body being "breathed" became an intriguing new experience. After one particularly revealing meditation practice, I recalled this experience in my meditation journal:

"My mind was still, and my body worked all on its own. I felt the synergy between the two for the first time in my life. Being absorbed in the moment sent a deep sense of blissful peace throughout my mind and body. It was incredible and the cheapest medication I'd ever discovered."

Since meditation only occurs in the moment, you can find yourself doing any number of activities: running, singing, or even deeply connecting with a friend—all meditative, all with presence.

RUNNING UPHILL AFTER LOVE

In my own journey, I swam, biked, and ran my butt off to be with Ray. He was an expert runner; I could never keep up. I was always trying to become the woman I thought he wanted me to be. Had I slowed down long enough to catch my breath, maybe I could have seen that all I was really running after—was me. To top it all off, I never asked him if he thought I should be a running mate anyway! In short, what I really wanted was a fantasy family—a family that I thought was ideal with how I was raised. You know, the standard American white picket fence story?

Ray was Chinese, first generation to Hawaii, and I was an outsider to his family, and more broadly, to his culture. Being accepted and finding myself was my personal challenge, though, at the time, I didn't know it. It wasn't until we were divorced, did I feel shame about my failed marriage. My mother reminded me several years later that she and my father only made it to twelve years. I had at least made it seventeen.

INTERNAL CLAUSTROPHOBIA

This feeling of chasing is a common phenomenon associated with relationships. We begin to construct a new social identity to find congruence with our new "role." Whether it is as "teammate," "friend," or "spouse," these roles can quickly come to define us—rather than us defining them. If there is any uncertainty as to how we should behave in these new roles, we may shift into unconscious role-playing. This is where we shape ourselves to fit the environment we find ourselves in.

That's what happens in a majority of marriages. Concessions are made based on the other partner's preferences because we all want to make our partners happy. However, this can come at a high price: our own self-respect. We begin to conform to an entirely separate person from the one our partner married.

Peer pressure can be powerful. Collectively, we all undergo a sort of peer pressure in trying to live up to the societal norms and expectations of who we should be. These expectations are often based on little more than an idea, or social modeling of someone we witnessed "playing" our new role. In terms of giving us space, this "role-playing" can be quite hazardous to our own sense of spontaneity and freedom.

Sometimes, we aren't our authentic selves, only fragments of who we think we *ought* to be. The times we become self-conscience of how others perceive us, the times we have done ignorant things, and the times our family and friends have loved us anyway. Even when this is not the case, the best way to live, always, is by doing what is best for ourselves regarding our ethics and morals. This is what stoics call living an authentic life, and if we live an authentic life, we will always be fulfilled.

I now recognize that because I didn't know what love meant to me. I couldn't begin to expect Ray to live up to my empty expectations. I didn't have any specific criteria to judge the quality of our marriage. Instead, I relied heavily on the bias of my cultural understanding and upbringing. Remember, when you are willing to forgo your expectations and create something new, your entire life changes. How are you going to change your thinking to get what you want?

EXERCISE FOR LIFE: MY STORY

When I first saw the man I was to marry, he was on his racing bicycle, riding through the edge of the lobby at the Hale Koa Hotel to store it before he checked in for work. Ray was wearing a bright-colored tank top and some running shorts. His tall, slender frame was strong. The smile on his lips was friendly as he swung his leg over the seat to hop off. He was a local boy, brown skinned and very handsome. Later I learned he was first-generation Chinese to the islands of Hawaii. I watched him through the window of the flower shop where I worked and immediately wondered who the good-looking man was. My co-worker friend noticed my googly-eyed gaze and mentioned that her husband happened to be a valet at night with the bicyclist, so she would pass along the news of my interest. She also said that the man on the bike was a triathlete, whatever that was.

Raymond showed up the next day in the shop and introduced himself to me as Ray, thanks to a messenger the night before! I learned we lived just a block apart and we both rode our bikes to work. I asked him what a triathlete was and discovered he rode his bike much more than I did; he rode around the entire island in a day! He was in training for the "Kona Ironman," one of many races he completed over the years.

I fell in love with Ray almost instantly. He was kind, handsome, fit, and owned his own home and two cars. Plus, he had a great family, he could cook, and to top it off, we had "chemistry." He was exactly what I imagined my fairy tale partner to look like. The bottom line, I felt safe with Ray. With all these qualities, shouldn't a marriage last a lifetime?

Throughout the years, I continually worried about my inadequacies. Was I enough for Ray? I wasn't an athlete. I could never run as fast as he could, bike for hours, or swim several miles. After races, I didn't feel confident to share in the conversations because I didn't think my story sounded as good as everyone else's. One coach even told me my running gait was the most unusual he'd ever seen, as if I had to use the restroom. Unfortunately, I believed him, and from that moment on, I convinced myself that I didn't look good, which further diminished my self-esteem.

After races, Ray would often sit at the park and enjoy a few beers with friends. I chose to go home. After a while, I quit going to the races completely and just waited at home, often preparing a meal for him to enjoy once he got back. Although he'd call a couple of times to say he was on his way, when he didn't show up for hours and the food got cold and went into the fridge, I got mad. I felt like he loved his sports and friends more than me. What I had failed to look at was the fact that he was living just like this before I met him, and now I was expecting him to change to suit me. I didn't recognize that. While I loved supporting Ray at the finish line, I never liked to exercise. It wasn't fun, and my angry memories of having to ride my bike home from school every day lingered.

Thinking back, my relationship began to deteriorate when our son Macklin was born. Having a baby provided another opportunity for me to look at the dynamics of where our relationship stood and what I felt needed to happen to make "us" happy, not just me. The deep attention I craved from Ray but didn't know how to ask for, I received in the love I felt when I looked into my baby boy's eyes.

Another problem I had was with my body: it had changed for the worse while Ray's body stayed fit. I was envious; Raymond Woo had freedom as he ran with the wind. Meanwhile, I was stuck at home, breastmilk everywhere, making me feel emotionally taut, physically mushy, and totally unsexy. He continued to encourage me to get the stroller out and go for walks, but I wanted more—more of everything, except sports. Specifically, I wanted someone who wanted me first and everything else second. So, I guess I was not only envious but jealous because

I continued to think Ray enjoyed exercise more than being with me, even when we were out together! Really though, it was a lifestyle that I struggled to adopt, and in the end, I became exhausted, trying to be someone I wasn't. The truth was, it wasn't about him. It was about me. I had no idea who I was.

Everyone loved Ray Woo, so when it was finally time for us to split from each other, my friends and family asked me why. They said, "We love Ray—what's wrong with you?" or "What about Ray?" I wondered where all my support had gone. My father, George, in his unending wisdom, continued to suggest that I stay with Ray as long as possible, simply because he was a good man. Dad's encouragement was steady and relentless as he pressed upon me the goodness of building—not tearing down—relationships, even in their demise. It was all about peace. I couldn't say then why I was ready to divorce. At the time, I just knew I wanted more of what I didn't have, and it wasn't something I could explain because I didn't know what I wanted; it just wasn't the marriage I envisioned.

What I did know was that Ray left me armed with a strong, healthy body. My adult life has been infused with fitness from the day I met him until today; from jogging, swimming, kayaking, to trail hiking, golfing, and now, a member of a fitness club. I love the activity, so if you invite me to go horseback riding, or play a game of racquetball or Ping-Pong, you can count me in. More importantly, I am happy when I look in the mirror.

When I look back and ask myself how I benefited from my marriage, I am enormously grateful for Ray's attitude toward exercise. It was simple and a part of life. Excuses weren't even a part of the equation; it was just what we did. His love showed up in the ownership of his store for runners (Runners Hi) and a kind friendship we continue to foster. On occasion, we'd dine together with Macklin who by then was a teenager and still the love of our lives. As fate would have it, I found Ray Woo in Honolulu. I said I'd never have a child but thank God for Macklin and thank God for Ray. My life would never be the same without them. Today, I am a deserving, exuberant, accepting woman, playfully living my dreams.

INVITATION ~ DECISIONS VS. CHOICE

Let's check in. I'd like to redirect the conversation back inward for a moment, specifically, towards examining underlying feelings and beliefs that are keeping you locked up in emotional bondage. By being honest with ourselves, we can break through some of the blocks that are holding us back. The only way to do this is through looking at how we are living, and how we can actively strive to do better in our lives.

Ask yourself this: How am I really living? Am I living in true choice? True choice meaning, following your own heart. Are you creating actions that make you happy? Or are you doing things because other people want you to or because you think you are *supposed* to be doing them?

The difference between living in true choice and just going through the motions is powerful. It translates to a much more deliberate lifestyle that is created in Love and will take you to your highest purpose. However, without the proper examination and continuous self-reflection, it can be hard to know the difference between the two and exactly where we fall on the spectrum.

Look at what you are doing (or what you have in your life) and ask yourself the following questions:

- Do I really love this?

- Am I doing it to be approved by someone else?

- Am I not doing anything on a particular subject or in a specific area of my life?

- Am I sitting on the sidelines watching others do what I want and hating myself for it?

Now ask yourself this question:

- What are the times in my life I am the happiest?

Make a list of five things you value. Let the above answer be your starting point.

I value the following in my life:

1. _____

2. _____

3. _____

4. _____

5. _____

Decisions come from judgement calls that are based on our past experiences. It is an act of or need for making up one's mind. Choices, on the other hand, aren't based entirely on past experiences. Instead, choice is the right, the power, or the opportunity to choose. We decide on goals and we choose dreams. Are we in alignment with our dreams? Is what we say, what we feel, and what we do really in alignment with who we are truly meant to be? When we "be" who we are, then the possibilities of life become endless. Live your full life; start being who you are meant to be.

CHAPTER 5

Wanting Love

"It is as easy to create a castle as a button. It's just a matter of whether you're focused on a castle or a button." - Abraham Hicks

Desire is the spark that gets you excited about pursuing new possibilities. But desire can only go so far. Funny examples can be taken from the popular 1960's sitcom *I Dream of Jeannie*. In each episode Jeannie grants a wish for her master, Major Nelson, and each wish appears exactly how he's asked for it. In one episode, a camel shows up in his living room. In another, he finds himself at the North Pole wearing only his underwear. The point of the story is that desire on its own isn't enough and that his thoughts actually become things.

Wanting something is more in line with calling something into our lives. The desire for a new car may lead us to look online for listings but wanting a new car may get us to begin a serious inquiry. When we want something, our desire becomes the *vehicle* for accelerating change. In the words of Mary Anne Radmacher, "Stand often in the company of dreamers: they tickle your common sense and believe you can achieve things which are impossible." Let your life be inspired by others who are daring greatly.

CHANGE IS COMING

As you focus on this small thread of desire and it begins to grow, you will also notice there is more substance to the desire. There are greater levels of commitment to action. When the realization hits that this is more than just a small idea—the act of wanting to make it a reality will become your new experience. And as this occurs, you will be able to grab onto your thread, which has now grown into a rope. This rope is sturdy enough to allow you to get a good grip on the situation and pull in what you want.

Some people are highly skilled in *appearing* as if they do not need Love, do not want Love, or have simply gotten over it all together. Do not be fooled—this is all an act.

Making Love visible stems from the desire to want to do something that fills our being with peace and bliss at the same time and offers the same experience to others. As you grow stronger in your resolve, you begin to want to do more to bring this vision into reality. My point in walking you through this distinction between *desiring* and *wanting* is to show that there is a multi-tiered process for openness to all that you seek in life. Wanting is important because it takes us deeper into our vision. It allows us to finally make a choice.

Wanting Gives You Hope

Wanting gives us power because it is the power of choice that separates us from our past, from the choices our family made, and from the choices made by others. This is why it is important to have a pure desire before venturing into the *wanting* stage. If we are not grounded, ideas conjure up. When we are grounded, *we* conjure up ideas. Wanting without clear intention can lead you to an All You Can Eat Buffet of options—all as seemingly palpable as the next. You may end up in an obscure location such as Major Nelson in *I Dream of Jeannie*, and wonder what happened. This can be dangerous for obvious reasons. This is the difficulty with having information at our fingertips—all of your old relationships are a click away! Zero in on what you want and leave the rest to the Universe! Ask clearly and you shall receive. It is law.

Approval from Others and its Importance

Recognition for one's achievements is an innate aspect of why we do what we do. If we perform a task at a high level, some want others to witness their performance. However, when we discuss Love, people look for acknowledgement from others that would be better served if instead it came from themselves.

Wanting to feel something vicariously through the eyes of a loved one is nothing new. But it is also something that can be dangerous to your perception of self. The more that you place your self-worth in someone else's hands, the higher your chances of being disappointed when things don't work out in the long run.

If you are simply looking for someone's approval of who you are being, the first time that your significant other asks you to do something that you don't like, or disagrees with your opinions—I promise you, you won't like the way you feel. Resentment can move in on multiple levels. If your situation changes and things are not working out, be good to yourself. Gain your own approval first and foremost.

Acknowledgment can come from the actual work, being of service, real Love, and true appreciation for your genuine efforts. It's great that someone thinks you're beautiful or that you have quickly risen to the top of your sales team with very little effort. The acknowledgement of feeling someone's attention and appreciation is at the heart of what it means to make Love visible, but only when it is well-warranted.

Wanting is not entirely bad; it is a way for us to consciously manifest our desires. Wanting love is really an easy concept to explain because everyone can relate.

However, wanting to find Love and be loved for the right reasons are difficult to uncover; people often become enamored by the person's physical appearance or material possessions, overlooking red flags (e.g. a control freak, an ill-tempered person, a pathological liar). Don't fall prey to the short-term payoffs that await you around the corner.

When choosing a new relationship, make sure both partners have pure intent. Though challenging, it is worth the commitment. When two people are open and honest with each other, it minimizes problems and puts each person's mind at ease, knowing he or she does not have to second-guess what the other is thinking.

It is not enough for couples to simply talk honestly and openly. They must also be effective at getting ideas across. This means respecting each other's viewpoints and being able to reach compromises. For example, if one partner is introverted and the other is extroverted, the introverted partner should be willing to attend social gatherings a few times a month. Likewise, the extroverted partner should respect his partner's desire to spend time alone, as introverts tend to need to be alone more often than extroverts because being around people for long periods tends to drain the introvert's energy. Whatever relationship you are in, it is important to reach a mutual compromise while keeping your own cup full at the same time.

This exercise will help you find alignment on the topic of wanting Love. Remember, wanting Love is a beautiful manifestation of who you are as an individual. Finding genuine Love is about being honest with yourself as you learn to follow your own inner guide.

INVITATION ~ AUTHENTIC LIVING VIA MUSIC

Being honest with ourselves is an arduous task. While it should be automatic, our survival instincts work hard, through avoidance, to protect us from anything unpleasant. Seeking the truth takes time and commitment.

Listening to music is one of the best ways to unclog our mental faculties. By hearing familiar and welcoming songs, it allows us to identify what is bothering us underneath the surface by bringing emotions to light. Often the bubbling up of emotion can bring tears, a form of cleansing that sometimes only music can elicit. Listening to melodic or spa-like notes in the background is often helpful. Take time to scroll through an old playlist or check out what's new on your favorite music app. Spend at least fifteen minutes listening to music that brings you joy. Note in your journal how the music made you feel.

Chapter 6

Allowing Love

"The greatest and most important problems of life are fundamentally unsolvable, they can never be solved, they can only be outgrown" - Carl Jung

A llowing Love is the process that opens the door to all that you want to experience. When you give yourself permission to start the *allowing process*, you are simply encouraging the Universe to work on your behalf by giving you access to what you most desire. Rather than thinking of Love as something that must be found, persuaded, or even reasoned with—try thinking of Love as a permeating force in your life.

This is a lot like letting someone into your home. You may not know exactly what they're up to, or what his or her mission is, but you do know that they have a desire to be with you for a while.

When I first met Ray, I had no intention of marrying anyone. I was happy minding my own business, working as a clerk in a hotel flower shop. A handsome man rode through the lobby on his bike one day, and my girlfriend noticed my extra friendly gaze at this good-looking guy. The next day, Ray popped back into the shop. My friend told her husband that I liked the guy on the bike and the rest was history.

It was clear to me that the Universe had orchestrated all of this. Love was working out for my benefit behind-the-scenes.

ALLOWING LOVE IS THE OPPOSITE OF STRUGGLE

People have become so disconnected from themselves that they have no idea how to begin to *be* in a relationship. Due to self-doubt, declaring themselves as victims, and playing learned roles instead of being authentic, they have no concept of the freedom that integrity and accountability can bring. Like an ostrich with its head buried in the sand, we sometimes choose confusion rather than recognition of responsibility; we choose to keep our heads buried.

People who are questioning their roles, titles, and expectations write the two stories that you will find in this chapter. Most importantly, they are learning more about themselves through giving their perspective to others. By contributing to this book, they've begun their own inner journey, and taken the first step towards greatness. Brene Brown says, "What makes you vulnerable makes you beautiful." This is your touch point to a new beginning of discovering what is next for you. Could you begin to ask yourself what writing your own benefit story would be like and the awakening that would occur if you were to pen down your thoughts?

A SINGLE MOTHER OPENING A DOOR TO LOVE: STORY THREE

I met Owen in the spring of 1985 at a surprise birthday party. I was the single mother of two teenagers and had been out of a relationship longer than I had been in one. The fact that we ever met at all was one of those chance occurrences that would have never happened if every spoke in the wheel of circumstance had not been turning just right. Neither of us actually knew the birthday boy, and we both had been invited by friends. I had just returned from a trip to Jamaica two weeks before, and my feet were still floating about a foot above the ground with the memories of my first trip abroad. While in Jamaica, I had been treated like royalty by every male Jamaican, and I came home feeling very let down by the men I knew. I wanted to have that feeling of being admired and most of all, *desired*.

It was a Friday night and my friend, Marie, had asked me that afternoon if I would go with her to a surprise party. My first instinct was to turn down the invitation because house parties were usually peopled with couples and it would only reinforce my feeling of rejection. I finally agreed to accompany her, but went with a heavy heart, as I now believed that I would have to move to Jamaica to find the type of attention I desired. Looking back, I realize that I tried on every piece of clothing I owned when I was dressing for that party. Some part of me knew that my life was about to change because that was totally out of character for me.

We arrived, hid in the dark, and at the appropriate time, jumped out and yelled, "Surprise!" There were so many people in the house. After eating, I sat down to play cards in the kitchen. I looked up and this not-very-good-looking man was standing in the doorway, staring at me and smiling. I looked away, but he continued to stand there and stare. I continued playing the game, and when I finally lost a hand and had to leave the table, he followed me to another room and announced that he had arranged with my friend to drive me home. I disliked him instantly. When I finally cornered my friend, she announced that she was interested in his friend and begged me to accept the ride home. I reluctantly agreed.

During the ride home, he announced, among other things, that he was going to marry me. I sat in the passenger seat, steaming. I curtly announced that I had no interest in meeting any American men because I had been treated so well in Jamaica. He listened and delivered me to my door. I jumped out of the car and ran into my house. Good riddance.

The next night, the doorbell rang and when I opened the door, he stood there with two pizzas for my children and me. I hesitated, but let him in. As we talked, I relaxed and liked him a little more. He was well-traveled, well-educated, and every bit a gentleman. When he left that night, I decided not to see him again. It was all too confusing. The next day, Marie told me that my ex-boyfriend was throwing a big party on the weekend and I was not invited. That would mean that everyone I knew would be attending a party to which I had no invitation. I decided not only to attend, but to also show up with a date. For the first time, I called Owen. He quickly accepted.

When he arrived to pick me up for our date, I had become so agitated about the party and the possible repercussions of showing up with someone else that I was in the middle of a full-blown asthma attack. Owen walked with me up and down the street in front of my house as I struggled to breathe for over an hour. My panic finally subsided, and we left for the party. We had a wonderful time and stunned my ex-boyfriend. Owen never went home again. We married a year later in Las Vegas.

I was happier than I had ever thought possible. He treated me with the highest regard and waited on me religiously. Every morning he ran my bath, plugged in my curling iron, and always complimented me on my attire. He bought me anything that I desired. If I noticed an item in a store, he would surprise me with it the next day. We moved into a gated community with a golf course, and it even had a pool in the backyard. For the first time in my life, I felt loved and appreciated every single minute. However, everything had its price. He wanted to be the center of my attention to the exclusion of any friends and even my children. But I convinced myself that my children would benefit from his money and connections and continued in the marriage. After five years, he eventually left me. It was sudden. It was hurtful. I was lost.

For many years afterward, I craved the love and attention that he had lavished on me. I wanted it back. I would cry myself to sleep at night and call for him to return. In any new relationship, I quickly judged the man's treatment of me as lacking and cut any ties. One day, I realized that if Owen and I had stayed married and continued in the same manner, I would never have learned my own worth or how to satisfy my own needs. I had fallen into a zombie-like state. I was numb to the rest of the world and eventually to my own needs.

I learned to treat myself with the same honor and respect that I had expected from others. Owen taught me how it felt to be honored. It took his example to show me feelings of adequacy that I had never known before. I had to learn to honor myself in the same way that I had honored him, and I eventually did. Today, I am grateful for the lessons of my ex. Each day, I rededicate myself to honoring my own needs and fantasies. I do only the things that bring me joy and only the things that honor my chosen mission in life. I owe my ex a huge thank you for showing up in my life, disguised as a husband instead of the guardian angel that he turned out to be.

Pondering Points:

- Do you choose being treated like royalty over self-respect?

- Do you tend to overlook a potential lover because he or she does not meet your fantastical needs (e.g. being treated like royalty)?

- Have you ever been in a relationship where you were treated like royalty only to have it suddenly end? How did that affect you? Did it make you stronger or weaker?

The Late Bloomer and Hard Wisdom: Story Four

I first met him in the 1980s. He was twenty-nine and I was twenty-two. Sam was a successful artist; a catch, a dream in my young mind. I never told him how crazy I was about him. I figured he couldn't possibly be interested in me for anything serious. After dating for a few months, we parted ways and lost contact for the next fifteen years.

One night, a few relationships, and a botched engagement later, I ran into Sam again—he was with his two young sons. I was at one of my favorite restaurants, venturing out for a solo dinner after a five-day depression, having come to the realization that I would probably never have children. I was approaching my fortieth birthday. He introduced me to his boys, and we had a nice talk and exchanged phone numbers. "He'll never call," I thought.

A few days later, he did. A few *months* later, we got engaged. My dream from fifteen years earlier was coming true—I could barely believe it. We moved into a tiny one-bedroom house on private, historic land in Scottsdale, Arizona. His two boys lived with us part time. I knew their mother from years ago before she ever met Sam. She was quite stunned that I was going to be her son's stepmother—though not as stunned as I.

The next year was spent planning our wedding. We wanted to keep it simple, small, and affordable. I was forty after all. Sam had everything he needed—so we kindly asked that no one buy us gifts. I went along with what were mostly his ideas, which were, admittedly, mostly great ideas. I hoped my family would forgive me for only inviting the elders and my three closest cousins. Inviting the whole clan would have tripled the wedding party.

We were married November 17, 2001. And we separated March 12, 2005 and divorced the next spring in April 2006.

The first red flag went up the summer that I reconnected with Sam. I was in Maryland working on my master's degree and staying with an old friend who Sam knew and did not like very well, as I soon would find out. Rebecca had worked at an art gallery and ran in Sam's circle of friends. She knew a lot about him, which is probably why he didn't like her. During a long-distance phone call, he asked me if Rebecca and I were ever lovers (back in the day, he thought I was "searching" and still exploring my sexuality). I reassured him that, no, Rebecca and I were never lovers, nor would we ever be. I insisted the sexually explorative phase of my life was over. Closed chapter. He did not seem so assured.

The next red flag flew a little higher. Before the wedding, I was invited to join a group of girlfriends for lunch. Sam was none too pleased that he wasn't included and couldn't understand why I would have interest in going without him. The concept of being with just the girls was not one he could grasp for some reason. I thought maybe it was because he grew up with all brothers. After some troubling discussion, I didn't go to lunch with my girlfriends. This was the start of a series of missteps on my part. While this was my chance to stand up for myself, I chose the path of least resistance and told myself it wasn't worth upsetting Sam. I could see my friends another time.

The huge crimson flag flew high one Saturday morning. Sam's boys were watching cartoons and he was reading the newspaper, calling family members in Pennsylvania, starting his day. I was in the mood to take a walk along the canal, so I got dressed and ready to go. As I was leaving, I told Sam I was going to get some exercise and that he was welcome to join me. He didn't want to go and strongly suggested I stay at the house. He was visibly upset. Why would I want to go for a walk when I could be at the house with him and the boys? I was dumbfounded. I couldn't believe my taking a walk was even an issue. This exchange bothered me—seriously bothered me. I don't remember if I took the walk or not. I do remember this clash was the strongest indication, so far, of things to come.

In retrospect, I saw these red-flag moments as ways Sam wanted to control me. This need for control turned into mistrust, and soon Sam was disappointed if I had phone conversations without him in the room or if I communicated with friends via email. Most of my friends were suspect as far as he was concerned; to him they were all ex-lovers or potential lovers that I just didn't need in my life anymore.

The reason I ignored the red flags was because I felt, for the very first time, that I was ready to be in a committed relationship. The usual fears didn't rear their ugly heads and I could easily picture myself growing old with this man. Besides, in a serious, committed relationship, you work through your troubles, right? Unfortunately, he didn't believe that I was committed to him. He did not trust that I was capable of it, even though I was *married* to him—my first and only marriage. Maybe my idea of commitment was not the same as his.

My mother-in-law had warned me early on. She told me that Sam liked his own little world without intrusion from outside influences. Was I prepared for that? At the time, it seemed an easy choice: He lived the life of a successful artist in a nice part of town on historic land full of creative energy and very interesting people. We traveled, enjoyed a fun, fairly unstructured lifestyle except for during the latter part of the week when his two sons were with us. We found comfort in having a domestic routine of dinners at home once the boys headed to their mom's house—housecleaning on weekends and Saturday-night dates.

In all of this, I am far from innocent. My biggest mistake was not being true to myself. I got lost in Sam's world, leaving my voice, friends, and heart behind in *my* little world, which wasn't really all that bad. I wanted so much for Sam to love me that I ignored my true feelings, gave up friendships, and interests in anything that was met by Sam's scornful disapproval. Those things ranged from seemingly trivial (reading horoscopes) to devastating (breaking promises to old friends). I finally realized what was happening to me. I wanted to start over, get back to the real me, but it was too late. He could no longer trust me, claiming he didn't know who I was anymore.

My second biggest mistake was getting involved in Sam's relationships with his sons, especially his older son. I had no tolerance for their lack of respect toward Sam, and I stepped in when I had no business doing so—it simply blew up in my face. And when he started leaving me alone with them on our Saturday "family" days, it only got worse. The boys resented him and so did I.

When our problems became recurring disputes, mostly about my friendships and my past relationships, I realized we needed counseling. I knew that if the marriage was ever to survive, which I truly wanted, and if Sam was ever to trust me, I needed help in getting us there. Sam refused to seek counseling. He insisted we could work out our own problems. We didn't need a third party telling us how to communicate. His communication skills consisted of bombarding me with words, as if I were on trial, until I broke down in tears. Then he would soften, kiss and make up, and sweep it under the rug one more time. This, of course, did not work for me after a while. Eventually, I started seeing a therapist, and as I built emotional strength and saw what I was doing to myself, I found my voice again. My relationship with Sam's sons slowly improved; my relationship with Sam deteriorated.

The clincher was the big fight before I finally moved out. He said two things that I'll never forget: He was just fine the way he was and "did not need to do anymore growing." When I pointed out that I had always supported his needs, but he never supported mine, his reply was, "What support do *you* need?" Even after hearing that, I still wanted to make the marriage work. I thought moving out was the wake-up call he needed. I did it for shock value. But for Sam, it was the last straw. We were divorced a year later.

Today, I am still in touch with his sons and his ex-wife (she cuts my hair). The last time I saw Sam was to get his signature on legal documents and to collect my copies of past tax returns. He still talks to my mother, and I'm grateful for that. She gives him tortillas for the occasional plumbing repair. He was always handy.

The benefit of my X, the big, life-changing lesson I learned was this: You must love and be *true* to *yourself* before you can be in a loving relationship. We've all heard *that* before. It only makes sense, but why has it taken me so long to finally grasp this concept? Wisdom? Experience? Years of failed relationships? I finally learned that you can't change your partner. Oh, the poor fellas I tried to change over the years, Sam included.

Today, I am in the most honest, mutually accepting, communicative relationship I have ever been in my entire life. We've been together almost two-and-a-half years. Sure, he's not perfect, but neither am I.

PONDERING POINTS:

- Have you ever ignored red flags in favor of simply being in a relationship?

- Where have you noticed that you've caught yourself at the brink of losing control?

- Sticking up for yourself is tough, but it is a spiritual practice. Creating boundaries is vitally important for healthy relationships. Are you setting boundaries in your relationship?

Invitation ~ Eye-Gazing

Our eyes observe everything. So, what about when our eyes meet the eyes of another? Or what happens when you catch your own glance in the mirror?

Eye-gazing is a sacred practice. It is one that calls the watcher to be present and the watched to be at home with his or herself. When you allow someone else to look into your eyes, it can be an extremely private experience. You can learn so much simply by making eye contact with someone. I'm sure you've experienced this at some point in your life. But very few of us actually feel the deep emotions that bubble up to the surface when we look into our own eyes. When we eye-gaze we learn to get comfortable with ourselves, and this forces us to release tensions, fears, and anything else that comes up. We are also forced to *face ourselves* without the comfort of filters. This exercise will change your life.

THE PRACTICE:

1. Set a timer for five minutes. As you look into the mirror, focus on making direct eye contact.

2. As you look at yourself, try to clear your mind, and focus solely on breathing and maintaining eye contact.

3. Pay attention to any thoughts or feelings that emerge.

4. Jot down your notes on what you thought and felt.

Each day add two minutes to your practice until you've reached twenty or thirty minutes. This is enough. Some nights you will reflect on your past day and how you could have changed your actions. Other days you may wake up in the morning and need to get focused, find stillness, or set your mind at ease. In a month, after each visit (with the love of your life) you will find out more about who you are and who you want to become. You may find yourself grinning, or you may see tears slip down your face in discovery and wonder. Invite the process and accept whatever happens.

CHAPTER 7

Inviting Love In

"There are no short cuts to any place worth going." - Beverly Sills

I nviting Love in is the gentler path. It leaves the door open for yourself, another lover, or anything else that your heart desires to come in. It also isn't as passive because there is an element of intention behind the invitation. Allowing Love is the process of acceptance, of letting things work themselves out, and learning to allow your own self-love. **Inviting Love** is the process of intention, of knowing your desires and wants, deliberately accepting that they are perfectly realistic, and you are worth it.

If you can't find your truth, I know for a fact that LinkedIn in Honolulu has over 439 volunteer roles available and that's just one site with a broad spectrum to choose from. Learning to give without expectations is the gift of volunteering, hence, being of service will lead you to your truth. Taking time to give to others will help you discover your path in multiple ways. You will forget about your own needs, you may learn a new skill, make new friends, and even travel abroad and work on water wells in Africa. The list is endless. The point is to get out of your own way. Also, giving to others is the best way to discover who you are.

THE WOMAN WITH CHEMISTRY KNOWS WISDOM LOVES DIFFERENTLY: STORY FIVE

I can't believe that I am better today because of my ex, but it is true. I was introduced to Marty through mutual friends who thought we would make a good couple. *Ha!* The chemistry was always there and still is to this day. But what is chemistry without the mutual feeling of, "I get you?" I can remember kissing for hours, but I don't remember that he ever asked how my job was going or how he could help. I married the guy because maybe I liked him, the sex was hot and, oh, I got pregnant. Sound familiar?

My mom even thought I was doing the right thing, go figure! We had a great wedding, and everyone had a great time, except me. He shoved the cake up my nostrils and made me cry. I guess it was the beginning of what was ahead in our marriage—disappointment.

After our beautiful daughter was born, I thought Marty would want to be at home with us and do things together. However, I would get calls like, "I am meeting the guys for a drink," or "I got tickets to a game." He never came home early or sober. I thought it would change, but by the time our second child was born, it was a well-established pattern. I did it all myself with the help of my mother and brother. I had a full-time job, two kids, and a husband who was a child and an alcoholic.

Marty wanted to further his career, but never thought of mine, as if my being a life coach wasn't a career to him. He got an offer to change companies that required us to move to another state. For me, I had to give up my career, day-care that I trusted, and my family. For him it was a no-brainer: We'd make more money and I'd get to stay home in the middle of nowhere. That was *his* choice! Of course, *I* chose to stay right where we were because I had support. And you can probably guess what happened, right? We moved three thousand miles away from everything I knew. I ultimately knew I had to go and give it a chance, not for me but for my kids.

The outcome, however, was not pretty. Marty was depressed by the new job. It was not what he thought it would be, and I was equally as depressed. I wanted to kill him for taking us away from everything I loved and for isolating us. Every day, he told me he made a mistake and wanted to commit suicide! I tried to tell him it would work out, but we were in a mess. I tried to be the perfect wife by cooking, cleaning, and taking care of our kids and Marty. I made a life for us with friends and neighbors whenever I could and was involved in as many activities as possible.

Finally, I found my voice. It was after 9/11. Some old friends were going to travel to Cozumel, and I wanted to go, too. Of course, Marty did not want me to leave, but it was a matter of sanity for me at this time. My mother came to watch my family, so I could travel for twelve days. I had to go and when I did, I found myself dancing on tabletops and living it up. Something in my head just snapped; I needed to make a change. I came home and got myself a job. I love being a mother, but I cannot define myself by motherhood alone. Once I was back to work, I felt more whole and a lot more confident.

Afterwards, I gave Marty hell and he deserved every bit of it. I moved into the guest room and asked for a divorce. I believed I could live my life again, and I damn well needed to get on with it without him dragging me down. Marty was amazed at how strong I was, and so was I. This was the woman I had been. Where was I hiding during my marriage? I thought to myself, "I am back, I am woman, hear me roar!"

Four years later, I now own a second home! The first one I purchased, the two kids and I outgrew, so now we have a bigger one. I have a successful career, and the children are happy and healthy. The benefit of Marty, well, he is now a father. He has our children every other weekend and some vacations, and he actually has to be a parent. I do not do it for him anymore or make excuses for him either. We co-parent and make decisions together about school, health, and any money issues that come up. We split all the costs of raising children, and of course, he pays child support. I do not earn what he does, so it is totally fair that he gives more to support the upbringing of his own children. We talk about college for our kids and how to save for it, but we put aside for it separately. I love that they have their father for advice or just to go to his house for a change of scenery.

Now that our children are approaching their teen years ("Ouch!"), Marty is great about talking to them about what *not* to do, especially about his own mistakes and faults. I can count on him to take over if something comes up for me and vice versa. We tell each other about funny things that have happened while being with our children and help each other with discipline. He will stop by and help with homework or to take one of the kids to a practice. There's always something that he can help out with. I think we know each other better than ever, and I give Marty more credit than he probably deserves, but I am not keeping score anymore.

The benefit of the ex-husband definitely outweighs that of an actual husband because I can count on him without expectations. Wow, I can't believe that it feels this good to actually say that Marty is a help to me, but he is! When it comes to our kids, he is there for them, and I can count on him to step up to run them to a game or party. I would definitely say he has benefited, too, by truly becoming the father he would not have been if we were still married. I would not say divorce is fun, but there is another side to it, and I have found my ex to be my friend. I know he has not changed all that much, but now I don't have to deal with his criticism and tell him to leave *my* house! Marty respects me now and occasionally asks me out for a date, but I am not that easy anymore. I know what I want in a relationship and I am willing to wait it out.

PONDERING POINTS:

- Do you ever wish that you could go back to the way things were when a relationship was new?

- The narrator found her voice through taking a trip with her friends and daring to go, despite lacking her husband's *approval*. What positive choice could you make that would be good for you, despite other people not understanding or approving?

- Ultimately, the narrator was able to recover her reclaimed sense of self through rediscovering her own needs, such as going back to work. What could you reclaim that would help you make the most of your sense of identity?

Invitation ~ Possibility Board

- Search through everything that interests you that you can print out, clip, or cut that supports your wildest imagination. Let your mind wander to thoughts you would never have considered before. See yourself in a land of abundance like Dorothy did in *The Wizard of Oz*. Home sweet home.

- Use a poster board, glue, tape, or whatever it takes to attach your images to the board in any fashion you would like.

- Set it up in a place where you can see it every single day. Let it remind you of what is possible in the days to come, visualizing your perfect end result.

CHAPTER 8

Being Love Now

*"The most important trip you may take in life is
meeting someone halfway." -* Henry Boyle

The following passage has been used with permission by Makana, an award-winning slack-key guitar player, singer, and composer from Hawaii. He posted this on his Facebook page:

People talk about opening their hearts, but it is problematic to open our heart. Upon opening, worlds flood in, drowning the self in a mercurial abyss of primordial oscillating energies, hardwiring the consciousness into a physical nervous system: the central nervous system of life itself. Opening our heart is terrifying: it makes for vulnerability, invites the potentiality of fresh pain, threatens to uproot the lethargy of familiar aches and regrets long-ago filed away as permanent fixtures of our identity and life story, stirring mud and unsettling the pseudo-safety of self-sorrow. Indeed, opening one's heart risks movement—oxygen and nitrogen rushing into the lungs of clovers covering the heartland, threatening to feed the fallow soil of the heart with the much-needed minerals of those rare-earth elements nowadays only found in New Age books and crystal gatherings in upcountry Maui. Yes, opening the heart is not for the common person.

But you are not common. No. YOU are life personified as it begs itself to strip naked in the mirror before an audience of eternity, quietly wishing for total surrender to a higher power, summoning waves upon waves to crash you upon the shore of NEW land, NEW love, NEW horizons. You stand at the gate ready to board a flight into your deepest being, wondering how you can bear the expense of further carrying this no-longer-needed luggage, stuffed with the ill-fitting wardrobe of past relationships that mirrored your then-self-doubt and absent confidence. The only sin is the separation you have assigned it and to carry further is insanity. Drop it all, now. Open your heart.

I open my heart to pleasure and pain

There's a risk inside every game

The chasm we cross when learning to trust

Is enough that no love is in vain

So, open your heart

-Makana

This is important because the basis for self-mastery, is self-creation. The more that you can consciously create your life, the better you will be at bridging the gaps between what you want and the love that you have for yourself.

To experience Love to the fullest, try volunteering. Being of service is one of the best ways you can enhance your Love and joy and spread these feelings to those around you. Finding volunteer work at a local church can help you decide your favorite type of volunteering. Here are some of many things you can find at your nearby church: children's activities, baking needs, and collecting food pantry donations. Even if you don't have a skill it is always great to see other human beings helping each other, and who knows, you may discover a skill you never knew you had.

This next story reveals how a woman who dealt with trauma during her youth and a failed marriage as an adult manages to transform her misfortunes into an act of service.

A WOMAN OF FAITH: STORY SIX

My mother died when I was twenty-one years old. My parents were celebrating their twenty-fifth wedding anniversary in the church they were married in when my mother passed out in front of the congregation. By the time the fire department arrived, she was dead.

Three months later, I met my ex-husband at Fort Dix, New Jersey. We fell madly in love and he asked me to marry him eight weeks later. I said yes, and we were married nine months after that. When we met, he had just come back from Vietnam.

As I think about it today, I am struck by the fact that we both experienced traumas right before we met one another—him coming home from a war where he witnessed many atrocities and me watching my own mother die.

Although we didn't know it when we met, we also both came from severe alcoholic homes with physical, emotional, and sexual abuse. I don't remember talking about it because neither one of us had problems with alcohol, nor did we want to drop our guards. We were always on our best behavior.

Every weekend before we got married, he came to visit me from New Jersey. I lived in New York, so it was quite a hike. We planned our wedding and everything was wonderful. We found one another and were happy that we didn't have to think about our losses. We celebrated and had a beautiful wedding with friends and family. My father held me close in his arms when we danced to "Daddy's Little Girl." There wasn't a dry eye in the place.

My husband got a job in Pennsylvania, so off we went to set up home in a new state. Shortly afterward, I became pregnant with our first son. Jim was with me when our son was born; we were both ecstatic. I loved being a *mommy*, taking care of our little family. We went for rides in the country on the weekends and talked about our dreams for the future.

Since we both came from dysfunctional alcoholic homes, we didn't know a thing about marriage or communication. We worked hard on our marriage because we wanted it to work. Soon, we made a Marriage Encounter. The weekend was for couples with good marriages who wanted to make them better. We became a team couple and helped others in their marriages. I believe the tools we learned there helped us to stay married and raise our family for thirty years.

My first memory of disillusionment in our marriage came when my husband forgot my birthday the first year we were married. I was devastated that he could forget something so important. I cried so much that I knew he wouldn't forget it the next year (wrong). At the time, I wasn't in touch with my anger. All I felt was hurt. In my family, I was taught that little girls didn't get angry. I learned to hide my feelings, especially my anger.

My husband had many jobs over the years, and he hated most of them. At one point, he was unemployed for a year. By that time, we had four children under the age of ten. We applied for food stamps and welfare. He suffered with depression but wasn't diagnosed with clinical depression until years later. Even after he was diagnosed and prescribed medication, he often forgot to take it.

I tried to help my husband (fix himself) and I gave him advice. I didn't like it when he didn't take my suggestions or do it the way I thought it should be done. I had all the answers and my focus was on getting him better.

As I reflect today on our marriage and my part in it, I realize that I unconsciously attracted him so that I could take care of him and feel good about myself. I didn't have to look at myself and feel the pain that was deep within. He attracted me because he needed to have someone to take care of him and be his mother. When you continually focus on someone else and their needs, you lose yourself and what you want. I slowly lost myself over the course of the three decades we were married.

At forty, I went into therapy and began the process of finding myself and what I wanted. When I began, I didn't have a clue what I felt or who I was. The three unspoken rules in an alcoholic home are: *don't talk, don't feel, and don't trust*. I learned and practiced them well in every area of my life. With therapy, I began the process of self-discovery and transformation. It wasn't easy facing myself, my people-pleasing behaviors, low self-esteem, fears, self-loathing, and feelings of inadequacy all at once.

As I slowly learned about myself and where I came from, I began to change, heal, and grow. I needed to heal the scars of a lifetime of sexual abuse, neglect, and abandonment. I didn't know how to love myself. I continually looked outside for others to love me and validate me.

Many of us stay in unhealthy marriages because we don't think we have a choice. I was a stay-at-home mom when my children were growing up. I didn't have a career to fall back on even if I wanted to get out of my marriage. So, I didn't think about it and just stayed. Sometimes, denial feels like a good thing when you can't do anything about your situation. I closed my eyes on some of the ways my husband treated me. After our divorce, my friends and family commented on how condescending my husband was towards me. I didn't see it at the time because I didn't want to see it. I stayed stuck for a long time because I didn't think I could make it on my own.

As my confidence and self-love grew, I got stronger and healthier. I started to "see" some of my husband's behaviors that I didn't like and were no longer acceptable. I started to speak up and say what was on my mind. I started to say what I wanted to do and what was important to me.

I went back to college at forty-four. What a challenge that was because I was terrified that I couldn't do it! I completed three years of college and dropped out for a year because I didn't think I could write a paper (and to think—*I'm an author and wrote a book*). Eventually, I went back, faced my fears, and then went on to get a master's degree. Having a master's degree afforded me the opportunity to get a good-paying job for the first time in my life.

When I made the decision to divorce ten years ago, I remember saying to myself, "I don't want to be seventy-five years old and look back and think why didn't I do it sooner?" I wanted to live my life to the fullest, and I knew in my spirit that my marriage was dead and had been for a long time. The spiritual path of self-discovery and transformation was important to me, but it wasn't for him. Making the decision to divorce was the best decision I made for myself. I would not be the woman I am if I hadn't had the courage to move forward with my life. I have never looked back with regret.

I am blessed that I have four beautiful children from my marriage. Even though my children were young adults when we divorced, it was still difficult for them. They saw their mom moving ahead with her life and their dad still stuck in depression and negativity. For a long time, my daughter blamed me for the break-up and that was painful. She felt sorry for her dad and tried to fix him, just like I had.

Thankfully, this has changed as she matured and came into her own truth. We now have a beautiful mother and daughter relationship. I have forgiven my husband and pray that he finds peace and happiness in his heart. I have forgiven myself for my part in the marriage. I know we both did the best we could with what we had.

My life has changed dramatically since my divorce. I am not the same person I was back then. I am truly a woman giving birth to myself. I know who I am and what I want. I know I can have what I want and deserve good in my life. I've needed these last ten years to be alone, to find myself, and fall in love with myself.

Last year, my first book was published, *Simply a Woman of Faith*. My book is about the power of prayer—asking for what you want and believing you will get it. It took seven years to write the book. I spent seven long years agonizing over it because I didn't believe in myself. I constantly told myself, "You are not a writer, you are wasting your time, and nobody will read it." I needed to change my thinking before anything would manifest on the outside.

I visualized and saw *Simply a Woman of Faith* in my hands before it was ever published, and I am happy to say that my book has been very successful so far. I am retiring from my job of twenty years in social services to promote and market my book, as well as lead spiritual retreats and workshops. A whole new world has opened up to me because I said "yes" to God and trusted the process and plan.

As I reflect on the ten years prior to getting a divorce, I realize now that I was quietly preparing myself by getting stronger spiritually, emotionally, and financially. I learned to take care of myself, stand up for myself, believe in myself, and love myself. I am grateful for the thirty years of marriage and the many lessons I learned. I understand that I cannot fix anyone else and that I alone am responsible for my life and happiness. Today, I counsel women and help them believe and love themselves.

It's a wonderful life and I look forward to the next chapter—when my soulmate appears. It's God's promise; I believe it and so it is.

PONDERING POINTS:

- Sometimes we put things off because we don't believe in ourselves and our talents enough. In what ways have you compromised your own success by *staying stuck*?

- Central to the narrator's success was her determination to go back to school and to write her book. Many times, we forget our dreams when we have a traumatic ex-perience. What is a dream that you could rekindle? How could you start working on that dream this week?

Invitation ~ Be Still, It Works

Find a quiet place. Once you are comfortable, take a few deep breaths. First, breathe in calm thoughts through your nose. Next, breathe out peace through your mouth. When your mind is at ease, ask yourself the following question: "What is it that I truly want?"

As you exhale, focus on this statement: "I truly know what is best for me."

As you repeat this step, you will gradually find answers to problematic circumstances in your life. This may take days, weeks, months, or years to get the full answer. Nevertheless, being still, or meditating, will bring clarity, which is an asset in a world full of uncertainty.

NEXT STEP: VISUALIZE YOUR CIRCUMSTANCES

Pay careful attention and focus on what your heart "wants." Ask yourself the following questions. Write down your answers in your journal if you feel called to do so. The more questions that you ask yourself, the better rounded and complete your answers will be. However, proceed with your own intuitive judgment as to what questions need to be asked and how you interpret your responses.

When you are in a precarious situation that has a strong hold on your thinking, sometimes it is best to use the sage wisdom of Byron Katie to shut up your mind. Your brain isn't designed to help you facilitate peaceful living. Your brain is designed so that you don't get eaten. Ask yourself the following four questions to help your mind calm itself down, and then do step number five (not listed)—which is to feel better about the situation!

Is it true? (Yes or no. If no, move to 3.)

1. Can you absolutely know that it's true? (Yes or no.)

2. How do you react? What happens when you believe that thought?

3. Who would you be without the thought?

Eventually your mind will let go of all thoughts and you will experience a sense of peace and stillness. Your body will find a way to relax into itself and your entire being will feel at one with all there is. It takes practice and yes, it is doable.

CHAPTER 9

Making Love Visible

"There are two ways of spreading light: to be the candle or the mirror that reflects it." - Edith Warton

Hawaii is comprised of distinctly separate islands. The state has wonderful exotic fruits, volcanoes, and even its own language, Hawaiian. Although Hawaii and the mainland are different in almost every possible way—the cultures, Hawaiians' unapologetic love for Spam, no Day Light Saving Time, and tropical jungles—both Hawaiians and mainlanders are housed under one American flag.

In Hawaii, on the island of Oahu (where I live), the people are rooted in a way of being, which is entirely separate, and yet completely connected via spirit to the seven other main islands in the archipelago. They have adapted their customs and colloquial habits as a way of making their lives more in alignment within the greater truth of the islands: *the spirit of aloha*. Aloha transcends the societal norms of our culture. Steeped in American customs and ideals, the islands aren't as noisy as Chicago or as busy as New York. And while a million people are hustling and bustling around on Oahu, there is an element that feels carefree and easy. The people go out of their way to be kind to one another. It isn't just a mere coincidence that many people who visit the island are stunned by the friendliness of the people.

At its core, *The Benefit of the Ex* is about seeing how different sides can come together through similarities. Making Love visible is recognition of your thoughts, words, and actions. It is a way of being. Actor Jim Carrey said it best, "The effect

79

you have on others is the most valuable currency there is." When you notice that something is missing in your life, a natural seeking emerges. You must ask to understand what is needed for the next step in your future. You can do that by asking the Universe: *How may I be of service? Show me the way.* When you allow yourself to trust the process of your co-creation with the Universe, doors will fly open with opportunity. In Hawaii, this opportunity is called "Aloha" and it is a unique way of living. Like Love, aloha is an overarching principle. It can be a noun, verb, adjective and adverb. It is prescriptive, descriptive, and subscript.

> *Auntie Pilahi Paki, who was a "keeper of the secrets of Hawai'i" tasked several of her students to be prepared for the future when the world would collapse. She spoke of the time when Hawai'i would have the remedy to save the world and the remedy was "Aloha." In 1970, at a Governor's conference she introduced modern Hawai'i to a deeper understanding of "Aloha."*
>
> *A secret of "Aloha" is that a person cannot do one of the principles without truly doing all, and if you are not doing one, you are not doing any. So, to be "Living Aloha" is to live all of the principles.*

This is an amazing concept that really gets at the heart of what it means to be in service, and to be living from a place of truth in Love to further draw on the connection between this book and its natural relationship to the cultural influence of the Hawaiian spirit. To learn more about how this is so closely linked, pleased observe the following, which is an actual law in Hawaii!

> *The **Aloha Spirit Law**. The **Aloha Spirit Law** is an actual law "on the books" in Hawaii, encoded in the Hawaii Revised Statutes, section 5-7.5 and acknowledges that The **Aloha Spirit** "was the working philosophy of native Hawaiians and was presented as a gift to the people of Hawaii."*
>
> *§ 5-7.5 "Aloha Spirit"*
>
> *(a) "**Aloha Spirit**" is the coordination of mind and heart within each person. It brings each person to the self. Each person must think and emote good feelings to others. In the contemplation and presence of the life force, "**Aloha**", the following **unuhi laulā loa** may be used:*
>
> *Akahai[:] meaning kindness to be expressed with tenderness;*

Lōkahi[:] meaning unity, to be expressed with harmony;

Olu'olu[:] meaning agreeable, to be expressed with pleasantness;

Ha'aha'a[:] meaning humility, to be expressed with modesty;

Ahonui[:] meaning patience, to be expressed with perseverance.

These are traits of character that express the charm, warmth, and sincerity of Hawaii's people. It was the working philosophy of native Hawaiians and was presented as a gift to the people of Hawai'i. "Aloha" is more than a word of greeting or farewell or a salutation. "Aloha" means mutual regard and affection and extends warmth in caring with no obligation in return. "Aloha" is the essence of relationships in which each person is important to every other person for collective existence. "Aloha" means to hear what is not said, to see what cannot be seen and to know the unknowable.

(b) In exercising their power on behalf of the people and in fulfillment of their responsibilities, obligations and service to the people, the legislature, governor, lieutenant governor, executive officers of each department, the chief justice, associate justices, and judges of the appellate, circuit, and district courts may contemplate and reside with the life force and give consideration to the "Aloha Spirit". [L 1986, c 202, § 1]

This beautiful way of life is an everyday reality for most Hawaiians, and it's made possible to a great extent by their strong call to love one another, themselves, and to demonstrate that love through service. Service isn't just about serving other people. To be effective, it must also be something that you want to do for yourself. Some of the most moving work we can ever get done in our lifetime is on ourselves. No one said it would be easy, but it doesn't have to be hard. You can never give up if you want to create change in your life.

One of my favorite acronyms for GOD is: *Good Orderly Design*. Whatever you deem *your* point of view, it is your co-creation with the Universe that makes it so. We are not held back by the Love we didn't receive in the past, but only by the Love we aren't offering in the present. Looking at it in this way, it's clear that the choice is always ours. To act in Love in the moment, or to let fear drag us back into the past: These are our two options. Faith is about taking the first step, even when you don't see the entire staircase. Tailoring your life becomes the journey to enlightenment as you discover that the privilege of life is being who you are.

When you grasp the idea that you are always being set up for success, life begins to happen *for you* instead of *to you*.

The stretch comes when we ask, and the answers appear. Often, these answers show up in unexpected ways. Who knew that by being in a crummy relationship that I would move into men's prison ministry in the maximum penitentiary and correctional facility in Hawaii for nearly five years? I couldn't and wouldn't have planned this for my life. But the conversation with my mom changed everything.

The following Sunday I was sitting in the sanctuary at Unity Church of Hawaii, when they made an announcement that there was an opportunity to be of service in the men's prison in ministry. I thought, *Well, I know what to wear, I know about eye contact, I've taken the eight-hour class on safety, and I've been re-certified several times; maybe I should inquire.*

A month later, as things got worse in my life, I decided to call the church to inquire about volunteering at a men's prison. A friendly voice answered. It was Mari. She told me that she had been trying to contact me for the past six months because she wanted to know the name of my hairdresser. After the small talk, she told me she had a volunteering opportunity at a men's prison. I was scared. It was easy to go into a women's prison for some reason, but the men's prison really made me feel backed up inside. Mari said I could carpool with her to ease my nerves. It felt comforting as she and I began to develop a lovely friendship. Toni, the senior minister who had been serving for twenty-seven years, was also there, which also comforted me.

We drove down a relatively long dirt road. As the car wheels spun, they spewed red dust in the air, contrasting with all the greenery from the sugarcane fields. On occasion, a bunch of little, wild piglets would be along the roadside munching on fresh grass.

We arrived just before seven in the morning. Typically, there was a long line of cars—family and friends waiting to see their loved ones—but the prison staff let us through first because the line of visitors was long, and we had work to do. We drove through an open field, parked the car, and walked past a few single-story buildings to the dining area. It had picnic tables and a corrugated tin roof held in place by metal posts. This is where we met every Saturday. Anywhere from seven to thirty men would show up for a one-hour spiritual service.

When I started coming here on my own, I never thought I'd be so moved; helping these troubled men encouraged me to begin studying to become a Licensed Unity Teacher. I attended A Course in Miracles about twice a week. Soon enough, I was offered the position of the Education Director for Youth at Unity Church of Hawaii. A paid position! What a delightful surprise GOD presented. Good Orderly Design. Understand, that I am not saying you need to become involved in a spiritual movement. I am suggesting, however, that you find a way to be of service.

It is because of this experience, that I was able to grow into the multifaceted dimensions of the woman that I am today. "Being of service" has become a foundational piece of a legacy that I consciously choose to leave. Living in the land where a state motto was adopted in 1959 of "Ua Mau ke Ea o ka ʻĀina i ka Pono" is a sign for me, that I am in the right place, at the right time, right now for me. This well-known phrase is commonly translated as "the life of the land is perpetuated in righteousness."

Can you imagine living a life where you are free from guilt or sin and where there are visible signs of Love everywhere? Making choices daily and even moment-by-moment is how we change our lives. Choosing to be peaceful and living aloha is an exercise for life.

I "Lup You"

Love often takes time to manifest. When my former mother-in-law transitioned out of her physical body three weeks before her ninety-ninth birthday, I knew that when it was time for her memorial, I wanted to be sure to share. I had no idea what I would say but would allow myself to be spirit-guided for a change, rather than planning a speech.

After Ray and some of his family shared their feelings, he invited others to the podium. As I raised my hand, my heart beat wildly; I wanted to share something valuable to everyone. Ray called on me right away. When I got up from the front row, a calm washed over my anxiety. As I approached the podium, I was proud to speak about a woman who did nothing but *make Love visible* her entire life; it was simply who she was.

As I gathered my thoughts and stared at the one hundred fifty guests, I was touched by all the familiar faces, many of whom I had known when I was married to Ray. I celebrated birthdays, weddings, and a lot of Chinese holidays with these people. I cleared my throat and spoke. I told them how great a cook my mother-in-law, Wai Kin, was. "From day one, I never peeled a single shrimp in her home. I don't think she did it because I made a mess when I tried to peel them myself," I told the audience, "I believe it was her way of showing Love for me."

I also remember that, when I had become pregnant, I asked Wai Kin how to say "I love you" in Chinese. She told me that there wasn't a word or phrase for such a thing. I changed this around quickly; I didn't want my son, Macklin, growing up around a grandmother who never told him that she loved him. This belief probably came from my own grandmother who always told me that she loved me. Wai Kin began to practice saying the words until she finally got them right—well, for the most part; every time she said I love you, it sounded more like I *lup* you. It was sweet, endearing. "I love you too, Mom," I'd always reply.

Months before she died, I sat in Wai Kin's bedroom. "I'm ready," she told me. She meant she was ready to die, to be with her husband. A vehicle pulled into the carport. "Boy-boy here," she said, an endearing nickname she'd given Macklin. Carefully, she sat up in bed and called to him until Macklin responded: "*Yning-yning*." This call and response went on for a moment until he finally arrived in the bedroom. As soon as he did, he sat beside her and said, "I love you." Her reply was the same.

"Twenty-five years later," I told the audience as I summed up my speech, "I could have never imagined this gift; what I had asked for had finally come to fruition."

After I sat down, one of my mother-in-law's caretakers went up to the podium. She began to share that, as a young girl, she felt left out and alone. No one ever said "I love you" in her household and especially not to her. As a matter of fact, her entire life was void of that phrase until she met Wai Kin. The caretaker said she wondered how Wai Kin had ever learned this phrase. When I heard this, tears rushed down my face. Who would have known that I, so long ago, created this intimate butterfly effect? I miss Wai Kin.

In the words of Ralph Waldo Emerson, "You cannot do a kindness too soon, for you never know how soon it will be too late." This is what it feels like when seminar speakers and pastors talk about leaving a legacy: something transmitted or received from an ancestor or predecessor or something from the past that comes full circle, even after you're gone. This is a concept that I never thought of until I found myself in a self-development workshop. When the word came up, it sounded foreign and powerful. "Legacy."

Invitation ~ Show and Tell

No matter how shy you are, the invitation here is to take a video of yourself, sharing how Love shows up for you. Then look at it without judgment and allow yourself to absorb what you have created and experienced through taking ownership of your life and loving yourself and others. Uncomfortable for some, nonetheless, you should take the leap; you will find a deeper meaning for everything.

CHAPTER 10

Creating Your Change

"The privilege of life is being who you are." - Joseph Campbell (Finding Joe)

This book has shared many concepts and ways to express Love. What's important is that you take what you have learned and apply it to your life. This book is a dialogue, not a prescription. Just like the quote above from Joseph Campbell, the man who created the famous Hero's Journey, we must all face the privilege and terror of being who we are in the world. Showing up is half of the battle; the other half is accepting ourselves for who we've been as we progress toward a better tomorrow and work on living in our present today.

Invitation ~ Writing the Benefit of Your Ex

This is your chance to write your own story. Now that you've made it through the book, you can begin to put the pieces back together that were shattered from your ex-perience. Be brave, write with conviction, and focus on your own growth and healing. As you write, consciously take back control of your thoughts, feelings, and emotions. Make sure you focus mostly on how you've grown, rather than placing blame on another.

Afterwards, you may wish to print this out and put it in a file somewhere, so that you can revisit it after more time has progressed. Please use the guidelines from the other writers (for the stories appearing in this book) as gentle suggestions (reprinted below for your convenience). Feel free to use this exercise in any format you wish, so long as it supports your continued growth!

In a positive, uplifting way, your story must convey the greatness of why you see a benefit in your experience with your former mate. For example, rather than write, "Because I left him, I can be free of abuse," focus on how the experience helped you to transform and become the magnificent person that you are today, not how you are better off without your partner.

1. The feature must provide an element of hope or celebration, so the reader can share your joy and learn from your story. What did you experience that created a shift in consciousness? Your example should support the reader in seeing how their life could be different if they chose to see their reality in another way.

2. The piece must be written in the first person. Dialogue is *optional*.

3. This is your opportunity to share the benefit of your relationship with your former mate. Let your heart sing and your pen glide as you break-through to finding peace with your past and expanding it into a better present.

4. Write for as long as you like or as succinctly as you like. The important thing is not your grammar or flashy, poetic prose. This exercise is all about how it makes you feel and what new revelations you come to through actively writing about your difficulties and triumphs.

5. When you are finished, read it back to yourself twice. I suggest printing it out and leaving it in a desk drawer for a few weeks.

6. Return to the exercise after a month and see what new insights, feelings, or thoughts come up. You may be surprised at how much better you feel since the time of your first writing.

7. Feel free to add amendments or changes to your story—as it is just that—*your story*.

A FINAL WORD OF ENCOURAGEMENT

My heart's desire is that you discover what peace and bliss feel like as you learn to make Love visible in your life. I see your awakening to the glory of you as a manifestation of Love and the possibility for peace on "your" earth and our earth to be available for everyone. Let now be the moment your benefits begin to come alive. You are worth it!

AFTERWORD

No More Hand Holding... Time to Let Go

*"I will believe the truth about myself, no matter how
beautiful it is."* - Macrina Wiederkehr

I hope this journey has been revealing in the most useful of ways and insight-ful enough that you want the very best in your life from this day onward. Remember, true change comes from within you. Therefore, there is nothing I could possible say in this book that could magically transform your life. However, I hope, at the very least, I have accomplished one thing: inspiring you to become the best version of yourself. In the introduction, there was a list of three things that stated who this book was for:

- if you are ready to accept responsibility for your life.

- if you want to be happy, and not remain right.

- if you are ready to start the rewarding work of letting Love have its way with your life.

Yes, this book is for you if you accept responsibility for your life, which means holding yourself accountable—at all times, every time. No one has the power to make you upset. Remember that the next time you are stuck in traffic and you are just about to flip someone off or roll down your window and shout a possible four-letter obscenity. Before you do that, stop, only for a moment, and take a breath while asking yourself this question: Why am I getting upset about something I cannot change? Sure, this method will not always work, but with practice, it will work more often than not.

This book is for you if you want to be happy, and not remain right. In other words, is it worth ruining a friendship or marriage just because you want to be right? If someone does not understand your point of view, then explain it in a way they can comprehend. Arguments can be avoided if people would simply take the time to see the other person's perspective. Therefore, whenever someone fails to understand you or criticizes your opinion, there is no need to become angry. If you have a strong understanding of who you are, then you do not need your opinions to be validated by someone else. You may have heard the statement "what you think of me is none of my business." In short, to be happy, means to be free of trying to be right.

Loving someone else is difficult, but ironically, loving yourself is probably the hardest thing to do, as people tend to be their worst critics. Should you find yourself berating yourself, stop, breathe, and think: Why am I judging myself? Don't all human beings make mistakes? Is making a mistake wrong? How can I learn from my mistake? In life, the only competitor is you against you. This, too, however, can change; if you simply allow yourself to be who you are at any given moment, the competition goes away because you have learned to love your ego. I use Love in this context not in the superficial way (e.g. I love my car, my house, etc.), rather I use it in the genuine way in which you love your significant other. So, to love your ego means to appreciate it for what it is but realizing that you do not have to give into it. Instead, notice it as a part of you. Yes, loving yourself can be hard if you do not learn to love yourself. But how then can you genuinely love anyone else?

Once you learn to love yourself, you will quickly realize that life is not hard, rather it is your perception of life that makes it unbearable. In this world, things happen for no particular reason other than being the result of choices you have made. So, if you dislike your current circumstances, instead of becoming upset, figure out a way to change them. I hope that the invitations in this book, such as eye-gazing and journaling, have been helpful to you. Practice them every day. The more you practice, the more likely they are to become routine, a part of who you are. You will become the Love you seek to be.

Invitation ~ Givers Gain

If it is a quantum success you are seeking, here are a few more notions to keep you in the flow and on track towards consciously creating the changes you seek. We all want solutions, and usually, we are looking for a quick answer to massage our damaged emotions, fix our wounds, and hurry up and heal ourselves. For this reason, I have created a list of items to activate new possibilities for movement in your life. My hope is that you will at least try one of them, if not several, and check in with your results afterwards. If it's not working, do something different. If you are even considering something on the list, I applaud you. Eighty percent of your success is just getting here, and the final twenty percent is going through with the actions! Picture yourself in the Indiana Jones scene in *Raiders of the Lost Ark* where he takes a leap of faith by stepping out on the hidden path above the depth of the canyon even though he can't see it. He believes he can cross whether he can see the path or not. Get on the path and trust that the Universe will correspond with the nature of your song. Your life is waiting for you!

1. **Giveaway:**
   Volunteer and be of service. Do something nice for someone else: babysit for free, walk dogs for the Humane Society.

2. **Counseling:**
   Get support, guidance. Seek help to make changes and create new growth.

3. **Return to education:**
   You choose what you want to study. Grow new skills, have fun. If you are stuck without skills, education can change that.

4. **Find a new hobby:**
   Take dance lessons, go fishing, take up wood carving, or work with clay.

5. **Return to work:**
   Try a temporary agency; you might find a job that you would like to turn into a career.

6. **Give to yourself:**
   Body work includes exercising, eating well, trying a new hair cut/color, pedicure, facial, body scrub, or get a new tattoo. Or you could do a release of vow ceremony, do some traveling, learn to bake bread.

7. **Fill in the blank!**_____

With abundant aloha & grace,
June

Book June Dillinger to Speak at Your Next Event

When it comes to choosing a professional speaker for your next event, you will find no one more respected or successful—no one who will leave your audience or colleagues with a more renewed passion for life—than June Dillinger. Since 2006, she has been giving inspirational presentations worldwide.

Whether your gathering is ten brave souls or one thousand, in North America or abroad, June can deliver a customized message of inspiration or present her series (YOU) for your meetings, conferences, or C Suite of leaders. She understands people don't want to be "taught" but would rather discover ways to live a fulfilled life through her message and words of wisdom. On stage, in a meeting room, or a gathering place of choice, she shares stories of inspiration, achievements, and of real-life people stepping into their destinies. She wants you to know she will speak in a corporate setting with all your top influencers, in a jungle with your preachers and shamans, an NFL locker room giving team support, at women's yoga retreats in Amsterdam NL or for inner city youth just about anywhere. She is here for you.

As a result, June's speaking philosophy is to inspire, to be in the spirit of authenticity, and entertain with passion and stories proven to help people achieve extraordinary results. If you are looking for a memorable speaker who will leave your audience wanting more, book June Dillinger today!

Visit the link below to book June for your next event.

You may contact her by phone or email to schedule a
complimentary pre-speech phone interview:

www.makinglovevisible.com
info@makinglovevisible.com
Mobile: 808-330-5555

BIBLIOGRAPHY

Aeschylus. *The Seven Against Thebes: When a man's willing and eager the god's join in.* Scribe Publishing, 2017. Kindle ed.

A Girl Exercising.com. "Henry Boyle Quote." Accessed December 7, 2019. https://girlexercising.com/the-most-important-trip-you-may-take-in-life-is-meeting-people-half-way/

"A Single Mother Opening a Door to Love: Story Three." *The Benefit of the Ex: Making Love Visible When Everything Changes,* 2019.

"A Woman of Faith: Story Six." *The Benefit of the Ex: Making Love Visible When Everything Changes,* 2019.

Brainy Quote.com "Edith Wharton Quote." Accessed December 7, 2019. https://www.brainyquote.com/quotes/edith_wharton_100511

Brainy Quote.com "Joseph Campbell Quote." Accessed December 7, 2019. https://www.brainyquote.com/quotes/joseph_campbell_378372

Brainy Quote.com. "Ralph Waldo Emerson Quote." Accessed December 8, 2019. https://www.brainyquote.com/quotes/ralph_waldo_emerson_106295

Campbell, Ernest T. "Give ye Them to Eat." In *Sermons from Riverside,* 8. New York: The Riverside Church, 1970. https://archive.org/details/sermongiveyethem00camp/page/8

Good Reads.com. "Jim Carrey Quotable Quote." *Good Reads,* 2019. https://www.goodreads.com/quotes/8711567-the-effect-you-have-on-others-is-the-most-valuable

Good Reads.com. "Mary Anne Radmacher Quotable Quote." *Good Reads,* 2019.

Hicks, Abraham. "It is as easy to create a castle as a button. It's just a matter of whether you're focused on a castle or a button." Facebook, Accessed September 25, 2013.

Imdb.com. "I Dream of Jeannie (1965-1970) Episode List." *IMDb*, 2019.

Indiana Jones: Raiders of the Lost Ark. IMBd. Directed by Steven Spielberg. 1981. Accessed December 8, 2019. https://www.imdb.com/title/tt0082971/

Jimmy Larche.com "Walt Disney 'lacked imagination and had no good ideas.'" *Jimmy Larche*. Accessed December 8, 2019.

Lewis, Leila. "How to Be a Girl Boss." *Inspired by This*. July 5, 2011.

http://www.inspiredbythis.com/business/there-are-no-short-cuts-to-any-place-worth-going-beverly-sills/

Lifeway Men.com "No More Sifting Through the Rubble." *Lifeway Men*. September 24, 2019. https://blog.lifeway.com/leadingmen/2019/09/24/no-more-sifting-through-the-rubble/

Linkedin.com. "Honolulu." Accessed December 8, 2019. https://www.linkedin.com/in/the-honolulu-828180194/

Makana Music. *Facebook*. Accessed December 8, 2019. https://www.facebook.com/pg/makanafans/about/?ref=page_internal

Maya Angelou Quotes.org. "Maya Angelou Quotes." Accessed December 7, 2019. https://www.mayaangelouquotes.org

Quotes.net, STANDS4 LLC, 2019. "Carl Jung Quotes." Accessed December 7, 2019. https://www.quotes.net/quote/38231.

Say, Rosa. "Managing with Aloha." Managing with Aloha. Accessed December 8, 2019. http://www.managingwithaloha.com/

Schucman, Helen, Thetford, William, et al. *A Course in Miracles: Original Edition*. Course in Miracles Society, 2006. Hardback edition.

Spark People.com. "Macrina Wiederkehr Quote." *CJWordplay*. Accessed December 7, 2019. https://www.sparkpeople.com/mypage_public_journal_individual.asp?blog_id=4015798

Spirit of Aloha.org. "Spirit of Aloha Temple, Spirit of Aloha Temple: Botanical Garden and Bird Sanctuary." *Spirit of Aloha*. Accessed September 19, 2018. thegardens.org/aloha-living- aloha/.

Sufiuniversity.org. "Rūmī, Jalāl ad-Dīn Muhammad Quote." *Journey Home*. Accessed December 7, 2019 sufiuniversity.org/programs/ journeyhome2017/

The Merriam-Webster.com Dictionary, s.v. "vog (n.)," accessed December 8, 2019, https://www.merriam-webster.com/dictionary/ vog?src=search-dict-box.

"The Drive of an Ambitious Woman: Story Two." *The Benefit of the Ex: Making Love Visible When Everything Changes*, 2019.

"The Late Bloomer and Hard Wisdom: Story Four." *The Benefit of the Ex: Making Love Visible When Everything Changes*, 2019.

"The Woman with Chemistry Knows Wisdom Loves Differently: Story Five." *The Benefit of the Ex: Making Love Visible When Everything Changes*, 2019.

"Third Time's a Charm for a Retired Naval Officer: Story One." *The Benefit of the Ex: Making Love Visible When Everything Changes*, 2019.

Vortex Healing Centre.com. *Vortex Healing Centre*. Accessed December 8, 2019. vortexhealingcentre.com/practice-aloha/.

The Six Stories Reprinted (in Order) for your Convenience

Third Time's a Charm for a Retired Naval Officer: Story One

"Third time's a charm!" How many times have I heard this statement from friends and family only to find out that it did not necessarily work pertaining to my own relationships? In my eyes, this statement is normally said under a veil of luck, and I now realize it was not luck that enabled me to create the relationship I am now living and actively participating in. So, for the record, I am married for the third time—and yes—this relationship is unlike any I have ever experienced before. If it is not luck, then what is it about this relationship that is different?

I have experienced numerous relationships and two successful divorces up to this point in my forty-eight years. I experienced the highs and the dull lows of being in two marriages with women whom I convincingly blamed for my eventual divorces and ensuing personal bout with depression and counseling. I entered my first marriage with mixed feelings at age twenty-four. I distinctly remember the feeling of being too young. However, I was afraid of backing out of the inevitable trajectory of where the relationship was going. I distinctly remember that my gut was telling me that I should take a better look at what I was doing. I didn't! I failed to take active control of where I was headed. Essentially, it was as though I climbed in a taxi without knowing my destination and telling the driver to drive wherever she pleased. My entire role in the relationship was passive. I did not know where I wanted to go. After five years,

I exited my first marriage feeling controlled, abused, and feeling as though I was less than. I attended various personal and family counseling sessions, however, to no avail. At one point, I even experienced the embarrassment of the local police witnessing an altercation between us in public. Thankfully, the police merely spoke to both of us asking me whether I wanted to press charges. I declined. Relationships with women I dated after this marriage also seemed to flourish at first, and then after the initial period, the same personal feelings began to flare up. I was unconsciously acting out a vicious cycle of my jealousy, feeling controlled, and then being ignored. This pattern seemed to appear over and over again.

Ten years after my first marriage, I was attracted to a woman who very much fit the same physical build, personality, and familial background as my first wife. At thirty-four, I began a relationship with her, and ultimately, we chose to marry. Even though I experienced the same gut feeling, and even felt the same sensation of red flags waving in front of my face, warning me that I was making a mistake, I still chose to continue with my decision to remarry. The initial euphoria of being in a relationship with a successful professional woman who had children was amazing. For what seemed like a fleeting moment in time, I felt like I had matured because I was now a married homeowner with beautiful kids. Ah, but sadly this was not to last. The red flag waving I experienced foretold the feelings I was soon to encounter once again. After a year of marriage and experiencing the distance in the bed between us grow further apart, I was asked to leave. Once again, the police entered the situation while I was at the house, and I was asked to evacuate the premises. The only difference between the first and second marriage was that I was a homeowner and stepfather of two children the second time around. Otherwise, I repeated the same story. Was I destined to live my life repeating the same unfulfilling relationship over and over again?

Fast forward to age forty-four. I had just retired from the U.S. Navy after twenty-six years of service and was invited to attend a personal development seminar. I was informed that it might assist me in shaping the kind of career I could create after my military life. Intrigued, I attended the seminar with my main focus centered on a future career. Well, during one exercise that weekend, I had a personal experience that revealed to me why I have continuously pursued the same types of relationships, and why I repeatedly got the same results. By taking stock of my beliefs and values, I discovered how I wanted to be loved by a woman. I also discovered how I wanted to love a woman unconditionally. This was a very uplifting, encouraging, and refreshing feeling that I had not experienced previously. I took action on what I discovered about myself and since then,

I have continued to work on being the best that I can be. I determined why my relationships with women continually followed a similar path.

At the seminar, I began to take responsibility for my relationships that had failed in the past and I realized that the women I had been with were not bad people, as I had told my friends and family. I realized that my ex-wives were merely treating me in response to the way I acted and viewed myself. The story I created about my marriages was that I was a victim to their controlling, dominating behavior. Of course, that is what I experienced at the time, because I was unable to see it any other way. Subsequently, I chose to take time to learn more about me, and in the process, I have discovered that I am worthy and deserving of an amazing marriage with an amazing woman.

I took the time to view all the relationships I have had with women. My relationships with my ex-wives have proven invaluable in determining what kind of marriage I want to create. I am now very grateful for the women with whom I previously blamed, had found fault, and who I had spoken about with a forked tongue. It has only been within the last four years that I have really accepted my part and taken responsibility for both my actions and the inaction that plagued my previous marriages. I realize now that I owe a debt of gratitude to both women because it is through both marriages that I learned what I really wanted.

As a result of my growth, I took action and took stock of how I wanted to feel, how I wanted to love, and how I wanted to be loved by the woman of my dreams. This is another area where I benefited from my exes. I identified areas in my past relationships that I did not like.

Armed with this knowledge, I created my extensive list of qualities and traits that I wanted in a relationship with the woman of my dreams. I focused on how I wanted to feel in this relationship. And then, it happened!

I met the woman of my dreams through a most serendipitous meeting. While waiting for a chartered bus to take me from my hotel to a seminar in Northern California, I discovered that the last bus had departed early. With no taxis available in this small town, I searched for an alternate ride. I met an old friend who was getting ready to leave the hotel also. Around the corner of his van I saw an attractive woman approach. We had briefly seen each other previously for a total of about twenty seconds, ten months earlier, but hadn't spoken. We recounted the moment we saw each other for the first time, and we described what we were wearing. It was a mutual exchange of eye contact with absolutely no words spoken. We were drawn to each other from the moment of our first glance.

Spending the entire week at the seminar in each other's company, learning about each other, we revealed that each of us had written out an extensive list of what we wanted in a relationship. And the best part was that our lists matched each other's perfectly! Surprisingly, I met thirty-eight of her thirty-nine non-negotiable items on her list, while she fit approximately ninety-five percent of mine. I attracted the woman of my dreams into my life, and together we are now creating an amazing life together. We support each other in our own goals and dreams, and we create opportunities that have never occurred to me in the past. I have become more confident in myself and in my marriage with my beautiful wife, because of our mutual respect for each other, our ability to communicate openly, and our desire to listen attentively.

I had experienced the definition of insanity by reliving the same type of relationships and expecting different results. Well, I have done something different and now I am benefiting with a new and very rewarding result: a loving, passionate, unconditional relationship with the woman of my dreams. I now view my past relationships with gratitude instead of disappointment. Because of these past experiences, I am now living a more rewarding and loving life with a woman of whom I am extremely proud. She exhibits incredible strength and courage. She raised three kids by herself, attained a vice president position without a college degree, and loves working with people. Together we are making a difference in the world.

I am no longer sitting in a taxi not knowing where I am going. My wife and I are in our own vehicle with our dreams and goals, following a roadmap of passion, fun, and fulfillment. We are truly happy together, living life to the fullest. We know that there is no limit to where we can go, what we can achieve, and how many people we can touch with unconditional love.

THE DRIVE OF AN AMBITIOUS WOMAN: STORY TWO

What is the *benefit* of my ex? The benefits begin with the knowledge that I can't expect to find something in a relationship that I haven't brought to it, which required me to take a look at how I was showing up in my past relationships. It also taught me one of the ultimate lessons in life: how to forgive. Not only did I have to forgive him for the choices he made, I had to forgive myself, too. The benefit that I received came in how I *chose* to feel about what happened.

My story begins like any other, filled with chemistry and romance and the appearance of all the right ingredients for a happy life together. Jason and I met when I was twenty years old, at a time in my life when I was absolutely sure I knew it all. I was so sure of this because I had already been married once before, knew what did and did not work in that relationship, and had a beautiful two-year-old son, Tyler.

I approached this new relationship with caution and a strong desire to make sure it was going to work before taking the plunge a second time. We dated and lived together for two years before deciding to make it official. Shortly after we were married, I applied and was accepted into the RN Program at a local university. This meant school full-time in addition to the forty hours a week I was already working to help support our new family. I knew it would be a balancing act to manage this hectic schedule, but I have always been eager to take on a challenge, and Jason had proven himself to be a great stepfather to Tyler. I knew that someday the sacrifice would be worth the temporary inconvenience.

I jumped head-first into my new roles. I committed, and I was determined to be the best I could be. Unfortunately, my school and clinical hours required a much greater commitment than I could have ever imagined. I remember waking up at 5:00 a.m. to get to school and staying up to do homework until after midnight. To be honest, most of that time in my life is a blur, like a picture out of focus. I am sure it is to protect myself from reliving something I barely made it through the first time.

To keep my sanity during this crazy time, I started running more and decided I would train to run a marathon. Again, Jason was supportive of whatever I wanted. He stepped up and took over caring for Tyler and for himself. I couldn't have made it through that time in my life without his love and support.

Life, and our relationship, started to slowly change. At the time, I was so busy *doing* that I forgot how to *be*. Time passed, and we quit spending time together. We quit communicating. We quit meeting each other's needs, and we rarely had sex. I quit bringing to the relationship what I still expected, or hoped, he would bring. I was just trying to survive, and I hoped that someday it would be better.

Two years later, with graduation one day away and a new house under construction, I could taste the victory. I had not only survived but conquered! I was graduating Phi Kappa Phi, the top 5% of my class, and was about to have my life back. What a tremendous feeling of accomplishment and relief! I couldn't believe it was finally over.

I guess that is why I never saw it coming. Finding out he had an affair was like being broadsided by something unimaginable. *It wasn't fair.* Why now, when I was so close to having my life back? Why me? What had I done to deserve this? There were so many questions, and nothing made sense. The worst part was that the affair was with someone very close to me, and she was pregnant. I remember feeling completely disoriented, like I had just been dropped in the middle of a foreign country where no one spoke my language, where I understood nothing—completely out of control. I don't remember my graduation, or if I even went.

Even though I felt betrayed, I wanted my life back. I had worked too hard to see it all fall apart now. I decided to work on forgiving him and attempted to make it work. We went to Tahiti for my graduation trip, a chance to get away and forget about the problems back home. During the trip, I found out about another affair he had with someone I had also known and trusted for a long time. That was when I lost it.

We returned home, and I filed for divorce. I turned to alcohol and more marathon training in my attempt to escape the pain. It was too much to deal with, so I just ran from my problems and hoped they would magically go away on their own. The problem is, I not only ran away from him but from everyone else I cared about. If I put enough distance between myself and everyone else, I would never have to worry about being hurt like that again. It was always there, just under the surface, waiting. I didn't face the pain of that relationship until years later, when I was married again and on the verge of my third divorce.

That was when I finally allowed it to hit me. It felt like a ton of bricks had fallen from a twenty-story building, completely crushing me. I had to allow myself to feel the pain of it all, to acknowledge that it had happened, if I ever wanted to be free. I spent countless hours devoted to personal growth to accept what had happened and the role that I had played. Through this process, I realized that I was not the victim, though I had played this role well over the past ten years. I made choices every day that defined the life I was living. Every step along the way I had a choice regarding the decisions I made, the activities I participated in, and the way I chose to live my life.

These experiences have helped define the woman I am today. I know, without a doubt, that working through the challenges I faced in our relationship helped me to embrace what it means to forgive. I will forever be grateful to him, the relationship, and the opportunity I was provided to grow!

A SINGLE MOTHER OPENING A DOOR TO LOVE: STORY THREE

I met Owen in the spring of 1985 at a surprise birthday party. I was the single mother of two teenagers and had been out of a relationship longer than I had been in one. The fact that we ever met at all was one of those chance occurrences that would have never happened if every spoke in the wheel of circumstance had not been turning just right. Neither of us actually knew the birthday boy, and we both had been invited by friends. I had just returned from a trip to Jamaica two weeks before, and my feet were still floating about a foot above the ground with the memories of my first trip abroad. While in Jamaica, I had been treated like royalty by every male Jamaican, and I came home feeling very let down by the men I knew. I wanted to have that feeling of being admired and most of all, *desired*.

It was a Friday night and my friend, Marie, had asked me that afternoon if I would go with her to a surprise party. My first instinct was to turn down the invitation because house parties were usually peopled with couples and it would only reinforce my feeling of rejection. I finally agreed to accompany her, but went with a heavy heart, as I now believed that I would have to move to Jamaica to find the type of attention I desired. Looking back, I realize that I tried on every piece of clothing I owned when I was dressing for that party. Some part of me knew that my life was about to change because that was totally out of character for me.

We arrived, hid in the dark, and at the appropriate time, jumped out and yelled, "Surprise!" There were so many people in the house. After eating, I sat down to play cards in the kitchen. I looked up and this not-very-good-looking man was standing in the doorway, staring at me and smiling. I looked away, but he continued to stand there and stare. I continued playing the game, and when I finally lost a hand and had to leave the table, he followed me to another room and announced that he had arranged with my friend to drive me home. I disliked him instantly. When I finally cornered my friend, she announced that she was interested in his friend and begged me to accept the ride home. I reluctantly agreed.

During the ride home, he announced, among other things, that he was going to marry me. I sat in the passenger seat, steaming. I curtly announced that I had no interest in meeting any American men because I had been treated so well in Jamaica. He listened and delivered me to my door. I jumped out of the car and ran into my house. Good riddance.

The next night, the doorbell rang and when I opened the door, he stood there with two pizzas for my children and me. I hesitated, but let him in. As we talked, I relaxed and liked him a little more. He was well-traveled, well-educated, and every bit a gentleman. When he left that night, I decided not to see him again. It was all too confusing. The next day, Marie told me that my ex-boyfriend was throwing a big party on the weekend and I was not invited. That would mean that everyone I knew would be attending a party to which I had no invitation. I decided not only to attend, but to also show up with a date. For the first time, I called Owen. He quickly accepted.

When he arrived to pick me up for our date, I had become so agitated about the party and the possible repercussions of showing up with someone else that I was in the middle of a full-blown asthma attack. Owen walked with me up and down the street in front of my house as I struggled to breathe for over an hour. My panic finally subsided, and we left for the party. We had a wonderful time and stunned my ex-boyfriend. Owen never went home again. We married a year later in Las Vegas.

I was happier than I had ever thought possible. He treated me with the highest regard and waited on me religiously. Every morning he ran my bath, plugged in my curling iron, and always complimented me on my attire. He bought me anything that I desired. If I noticed an item in a store, he would surprise me with it the next day. We moved into a gated community with a golf course, and it even had a pool in the backyard. For the first time in my life, I felt loved and appreciated every single minute. However, everything had its price. He wanted to be the center of my attention to the exclusion of any friends and even my children. But I convinced myself that my children would benefit from his money and connections and continued in the marriage. After five years, he eventually left me. It was sudden. It was hurtful. I was lost.

For many years afterward, I craved the love and attention that he had lavished on me. I wanted it back. I would cry myself to sleep at night and call for him to return. In any new relationship, I quickly judged the man's treatment of me as lacking and cut any ties. One day, I realized that if Owen and I had stayed married and continued in the same manner, I would never have learned my own worth or how to satisfy my own needs. I had fallen into a zombie-like state. I was numb to the rest of the world and eventually to my own needs.

I learned to treat myself with the same honor and respect that I had expected from others. Owen taught me how it felt to be honored. It took his example to show me feelings of adequacy that I had never known before. I had to learn to honor myself in the same way that I had honored him, and I eventually did. Today, I am grateful for the lessons of my ex. Each day, I rededicate myself to honoring my own needs and fantasies. I do only the things that bring me joy and only the things that honor my chosen mission in life. I owe my ex a huge thank you for showing up in my life, disguised as a husband instead of the guardian angel that he turned out to be.

THE LATE BLOOMER AND HARD WISDOM: STORY FOUR

I first met him in the 1980s. He was twenty-nine and I was twenty-two. Sam was a successful artist; a catch, a dream in my young mind. I never told him how crazy I was about him. I figured he couldn't possibly be interested in me for anything serious. After dating for a few months, we parted ways and lost contact for the next fifteen years.

One night, a few relationships, and a botched engagement later, I ran into Sam again—he was with his two young sons. I was at one of my favorite restaurants, venturing out for a solo dinner after a five-day depression, having come to the realization that I would probably never have children. I was approaching my fortieth birthday. He introduced me to his boys, and we had a nice talk and exchanged phone numbers. "He'll never call," I thought.

A few days later, he did. A few *months* later, we got engaged. My dream from fifteen years earlier was coming true—I could barely believe it. We moved into a tiny one-bedroom house on private, historic land in Scottsdale, Arizona. His two boys lived with us part time. I knew their mother from years ago before she ever met Sam. She was quite stunned that I was going to be her son's stepmother—though not as stunned as I.

The next year was spent planning our wedding. We wanted to keep it simple, small, and affordable. I was forty after all. Sam had everything he needed—so we kindly asked that no one buy us gifts. I went along with what were mostly his ideas, which were, admittedly, mostly great ideas. I hoped my family would forgive me for only inviting the elders and my three closest cousins. Inviting the whole clan would have tripled the wedding party.

We were married November 17, 2001. And we separated March 12, 2005 and divorced the next spring in April 2006.

The first red flag went up the summer that I reconnected with Sam. I was in Maryland working on my master's degree and staying with an old friend who Sam knew and did not like very well, as I soon would find out. Rebecca had worked at an art gallery and ran in Sam's circle of friends. She knew a lot about him, which is probably why he didn't like her. During a long-distance phone call, he asked me if Rebecca and I were ever lovers (back in the day, he thought I was "searching" and still exploring my sexuality). I reassured him that, no, Rebecca and I were never lovers, nor would we ever be. I insisted the sexually explorative phase of my life was over. Closed chapter. He did not seem so assured.

The next red flag flew a little higher. Before the wedding, I was invited to join a group of girlfriends for lunch. Sam was none too pleased that he wasn't included and couldn't understand why I would have interest in going without him. The concept of being with just the girls was not one he could grasp for some reason. I thought maybe it was because he grew up with all brothers. After some troubling discussion, I didn't go to lunch with my girlfriends. This was the start of a series of missteps on my part. While this was my chance to stand up for myself, I chose the path of least resistance and told myself it wasn't worth upsetting Sam. I could see my friends another time.

The huge crimson flag flew high one Saturday morning. Sam's boys were watching cartoons and he was reading the newspaper, calling family members in Pennsylvania, starting his day. I was in the mood to take a walk along the canal, so I got dressed and ready to go. As I was leaving, I told Sam I was going to get some exercise and that he was welcome to join me. He didn't want to go and strongly suggested I stay at the house. He was visibly upset. Why would I want to go for a walk when I could be at the house with him and the boys? I was dumbfounded. I couldn't believe my taking a walk was even an issue. This exchange bothered me—seriously bothered me. I don't remember if I took the walk or not. I do remember this clash was the strongest indication, so far, of things to come.

In retrospect, I saw these red-flag moments as ways Sam wanted to control me. This need for control turned into mistrust, and soon Sam was disappointed if I had phone conversations without him in the room or if I communicated with friends via email. Most of my friends were suspect as far as he was concerned; to him they were all ex-lovers or potential lovers that I just didn't need in my life anymore.

The reason I ignored the red flags was because I felt, for the very first time, that I was ready to be in a committed relationship. The usual fears didn't rear their ugly heads and I could easily picture myself growing old with this man. Besides, in a serious, committed relationship, you work through your troubles, right? Unfortunately, he didn't believe that I was committed to him. He did not trust that I was capable of it, even though I was *married* to him—my first and only marriage. Maybe my idea of commitment was not the same as his.

My mother-in-law had warned me early on. She told me that Sam liked his own little world without intrusion from outside influences. Was I prepared for that? At the time, it seemed an easy choice: He lived the life of a successful artist in a nice part of town on historic land full of creative energy and very interesting people. We traveled, enjoyed a fun, fairly unstructured lifestyle except for during the latter part of the week when his two sons were with us. We found comfort in having a domestic routine of dinners at home once the boys headed to their mom's house—housecleaning on weekends and Saturday-night dates.

In all of this, I am far from innocent. My biggest mistake was not being true to myself. I got lost in Sam's world, leaving my voice, friends, and heart behind in *my* little world, which wasn't really all that bad. I wanted so much for Sam to love me that I ignored my true feelings, gave up friendships, and interests in anything that was met by Sam's scornful disapproval. Those things ranged from seemingly trivial (reading horoscopes) to devastating (breaking promises to old friends). I finally realized what was happening to me. I wanted to start over, get back to the real me, but it was too late. He could no longer trust me, claiming he didn't know who I was anymore.

My second biggest mistake was getting involved in Sam's relationships with his sons, especially his older son. I had no tolerance for their lack of respect toward Sam, and I stepped in when I had no business doing so—it simply blew up in my face. And when he started leaving me alone with them on our Saturday "family" days, it only got worse. The boys resented him and so did I.

When our problems became recurring disputes, mostly about my friendships and my past relationships, I realized we needed counseling. I knew that if the marriage was ever to survive, which I truly wanted, and if Sam was ever to trust me, I needed help in getting us there. Sam refused to seek counseling. He insisted we could work out our own problems. We didn't need a third party telling us how to communicate. His communication skills consisted of bombarding me with words, as if I were on trial, until I broke down in tears. Then he would soften, kiss and make up, and sweep it under the rug one more time. This, of course, did not work for me after a while. Eventually, I started seeing a therapist, and as I built emotional strength and saw what I was doing to myself, I found my voice again. My relationship with Sam's sons slowly improved; my relationship with Sam deteriorated.

The clincher was the big fight before I finally moved out. He said two things that I'll never forget: He was just fine the way he was and "did not need to do anymore growing." When I pointed out that I had always supported his needs, but he never supported mine, his reply was, "What support do *you* need?" Even after hearing that, I still wanted to make the marriage work. I thought moving out was the wake-up call he needed. I did it for shock value. But for Sam, it was the last straw. We were divorced a year later.

Today, I am still in touch with his sons and his ex-wife (she cuts my hair). The last time I saw Sam was to get his signature on legal documents and to collect my copies of past tax returns. He still talks to my mother, and I'm grateful for that. She gives him tortillas for the occasional plumbing repair. He was always handy.

The benefit of my X, the big, life-changing lesson I learned was this: You must love and be *true* to *yourself* before you can be in a loving relationship. We've all heard *that* before. It only makes sense, but why has it taken me so long to finally grasp this concept? Wisdom? Experience? Years of failed relationships? I finally learned that you can't change your partner. Oh, the poor fellas I tried to change over the years, Sam included.

Today, I am in the most honest, mutually accepting, communicative relationship I have ever been in my entire life. We've been together almost two-and-a-half years. Sure, he's not perfect, but neither am I.

THE WOMAN WITH CHEMISTRY KNOWS WISDOM LOVES DIFFERENTLY: STORY FIVE

I can't believe that I am better today because of my ex, but it is true. I was introduced to Marty through mutual friends who thought we would make a good couple. *Ha!* The chemistry was always there and still is to this day. But what is chemistry without the mutual feeling of, "I get you?" I can remember kissing for hours, but I don't remember that he ever asked how my job was going or how he could help. I married the guy because maybe I liked him, the sex was hot and, oh, I got pregnant. Sound familiar?

My mom even thought I was doing the right thing, go figure! We had a great wedding, and everyone had a great time, except me. He shoved the cake up my nostrils and made me cry. I guess it was the beginning of what was ahead in our marriage—disappointment.

After our beautiful daughter was born, I thought Marty would want to be at home with us and do things together. However, I would get calls like, "I am meeting the guys for a drink," or "I got tickets to a game." He never came home early or sober. I thought it would change, but by the time our second child was born, it was a well-established pattern. I did it all myself with the help of my mother and brother. I had a full-time job, two kids, and a husband who was a child and an alcoholic.

Marty wanted to further his career, but never thought of mine, as if my being a life coach wasn't a career to him. He got an offer to change companies that required us to move to another state. For me, I had to give up my career, daycare that I trusted, and my family. For him it was a no-brainer: We'd make more money and I'd get to stay home in the middle of nowhere. That was *his* choice! Of course, *I* chose to stay right where we were because I had support. And you can probably guess what happened, right? We moved three thousand miles away from everything I knew. I ultimately knew I had to go and give it a chance, not for me but for my kids.

The outcome, however, was not pretty. Marty was depressed by the new job. It was not what he thought it would be, and I was equally as depressed. I wanted to kill him for taking us away from everything I loved and for isolating us. Every day, he told me he made a mistake and wanted to commit suicide! I tried to tell him it would work out, but we were in a mess. I tried to be the perfect wife by cooking, cleaning, and taking care of our kids and Marty. I made a life for us with friends and neighbors whenever I could and was involved in as many activities as possible.

Finally, I found my voice. It was after 9/11. Some old friends were going to travel to Cozumel, and I wanted to go, too. Of course, Marty did not want me to leave, but it was a matter of sanity for me at this time. My mother came to watch my family, so I could travel for twelve days. I had to go and when I did, I found myself dancing on tabletops and living it up. Something in my head just snapped; I needed to make a change. I came home and got myself a job. I love being a mother, but I cannot define myself by motherhood alone. Once I was back to work, I felt more whole and a lot more confident.

Afterwards, I gave Marty hell and he deserved every bit of it. I moved into the guest room and asked for a divorce. I believed I could live my life again, and I damn well needed to get on with it without him dragging me down. Marty was amazed at how strong I was, and so was I. This was the woman I had been. Where was I hiding during my marriage? I thought to myself, "I am back, I am woman, hear me roar!"

Four years later, I now own a second home! The first one I purchased, the two kids and I outgrew, so now we have a bigger one. I have a successful career, and the children are happy and healthy. The benefit of Marty, well, he is now a father. He has our children every other weekend and some vacations, and he actually has to be a parent. I do not do it for him anymore or make excuses for him either. We co-parent and make decisions together about school, health, and any money issues that come up. We split all the costs of raising children, and of course, he pays child support. I do not earn what he does, so it is totally fair that he gives more to support the upbringing of his own children. We talk about college for our kids and how to save for it, but we put aside for it separately. I love that they have their father for advice or just to go to his house for a change of scenery.

Now that our children are approaching their teen years ("Ouch!"), Marty is great about talking to them about what *not* to do, especially about his own mistakes and faults. I can count on him to take over if something comes up for me and vice versa. We tell each other about funny things that have happened while being with our children and help each other with discipline. He will stop by and help with homework or to take one of the kids to a practice. There's always something that he can help out with. I think we know each other better than ever, and I give Marty more credit than he probably deserves, but I am not keeping score anymore.

The benefit of the ex-husband definitely outweighs that of an actual husband because I can count on him without expectations. Wow, I can't believe that it feels this good to actually say that Marty is a help to me, but he is! When it comes to our kids, he is there for them, and I can count on him to step up to run them to a game or party. I would definitely say he has benefited, too, by truly becoming the father he would not have been if we were still married. I would not say divorce is fun, but there is another side to it, and I have found my ex to be my friend. I know he has not changed all that much, but now I don't have to deal with his criticism and tell him to leave *my* house! Marty respects me now and occasionally asks me out for a date, but I am not that easy anymore. I know what I want in a relationship and I am willing to wait it out.

A WOMAN OF FAITH: STORY SIX

My mother died when I was twenty-one years old. My parents were celebrating their twenty-fifth wedding anniversary in the church they were married in when my mother passed out in front of the congregation. By the time the fire department arrived, she was dead.

Three months later, I met my ex-husband at Fort Dix, New Jersey. We fell madly in love and he asked me to marry him eight weeks later. I said yes, and we were married nine months after that. When we met, he had just come back from Vietnam.

As I think about it today, I am struck by the fact that we both experienced traumas right before we met one another—him coming home from a war where he witnessed many atrocities and me watching my own mother die.

Although we didn't know it when we met, we also both came from severe alcoholic homes with physical, emotional, and sexual abuse. I don't remember talking about it because neither one of us had problems with alcohol, nor did we want to drop our guards. We were always on our best behavior.

Every weekend before we got married, he came to visit me from New Jersey. I lived in New York, so it was quite a hike. We planned our wedding and everything was wonderful. We found one another and were happy that we didn't have to think about our losses. We celebrated and had a beautiful wedding with friends and family. My father held me close in his arms when we danced to "Daddy's Little Girl." There wasn't a dry eye in the place.

My husband got a job in Pennsylvania, so off we went to set up home in a new state. Shortly afterward, I became pregnant with our first son. Jim was with me when our son was born; we were both ecstatic. I loved being a *mommy*, taking

112

care of our little family. We went for rides in the country on the weekends and talked about our dreams for the future.

Since we both came from dysfunctional alcoholic homes, we didn't know a thing about marriage or communication. We worked hard on our marriage because we wanted it to work. Soon, we made a Marriage Encounter. The weekend was for couples with good marriages who wanted to make them better. We became a team couple and helped others in their marriages. I believe the tools we learned there helped us to stay married and raise our family for thirty years.

My first memory of disillusionment in our marriage came when my husband forgot my birthday the first year we were married. I was devastated that he could forget something so important. I cried so much that I knew he wouldn't forget it the next year (wrong). At the time, I wasn't in touch with my anger. All I felt was hurt. In my family, I was taught that little girls didn't get angry. I learned to hide my feelings, especially my anger.

My husband had many jobs over the years, and he hated most of them. At one point, he was unemployed for a year. By that time, we had four children under the age of ten. We applied for food stamps and welfare. He suffered with depression but wasn't diagnosed with clinical depression until years later. Even after he was diagnosed and prescribed medication, he often forgot to take it.

I tried to help my husband (fix himself) and I gave him advice. I didn't like it when he didn't take my suggestions or do it the way I thought it should be done. I had all the answers and my focus was on getting him better.

As I reflect today on our marriage and my part in it, I realize that I unconsciously attracted him so that I could take care of him and feel good about myself. I didn't have to look at myself and feel the pain that was deep within. He attracted me because he needed to have someone to take care of him and be his mother. When you continually focus on someone else and their needs, you lose yourself and what you want. I slowly lost myself over the course of the three decades we were married.

At forty, I went into therapy and began the process of finding myself and what I wanted. When I began, I didn't have a clue what I felt or who I was. The three unspoken rules in an alcoholic home are: *don't talk, don't feel, and don't trust*. I learned and practiced them well in every area of my life. With therapy, I began the process of self-discovery and transformation. It wasn't easy facing myself, my people-pleasing behaviors, low self-esteem, fears, self-loathing, and feelings of inadequacy all at once.

As I slowly learned about myself and where I came from, I began to change, heal, and grow. I needed to heal the scars of a lifetime of sexual abuse, neglect, and abandonment. I didn't know how to love myself. I continually looked outside for others to love me and validate me.

Many of us stay in unhealthy marriages because we don't think we have a choice. I was a stay-at-home mom when my children were growing up. I didn't have a career to fall back on even if I wanted to get out of my marriage. So, I didn't think about it and just stayed. Sometimes, denial feels like a good thing when you can't do anything about your situation. I closed my eyes on some of the ways my husband treated me. After our divorce, my friends and family commented on how condescending my husband was towards me. I didn't see it at the time because I didn't want to see it. I stayed stuck for a long time because I didn't think I could make it on my own.

As my confidence and self-love grew, I got stronger and healthier. I started to "see" some of my husband's behaviors that I didn't like and were no longer acceptable. I started to speak up and say what was on my mind. I started to say what I wanted to do and what was important to me.

I went back to college at forty-four. What a challenge that was because I was terrified that I couldn't do it! I completed three years of college and dropped out for a year because I didn't think I could write a paper (and to think—*I'm an author and wrote a book*). Eventually, I went back, faced my fears, and then went on to get a master's degree. Having a master's degree afforded me the opportunity to get a good-paying job for the first time in my life.

When I made the decision to divorce ten years ago, I remember saying to myself, *I don't want to be seventy-five years old and look back and say, "Why didn't I do it sooner?"* I wanted to live my life to the fullest, and I knew in my spirit that my marriage was dead and had been for a long time. The spiritual path of self-discovery and transformation was important to me, but it wasn't for him. Making the decision to divorce was the best decision I made for myself. I would not be the woman I am if I hadn't had the courage to move forward with my life. I have never looked back with regret.

I am blessed that I have four beautiful children from my marriage. Even though my children were young adults when we divorced, it was still difficult for them. They saw their mom moving ahead with her life and their dad still stuck in depression and negativity. For a long time, my daughter blamed me for the break-up and that was painful. She felt sorry for her dad and tried to fix him, just like I had.

Thankfully, this has changed as she matured and came into her own truth. We now have a beautiful mother and daughter relationship. I have forgiven my husband and pray that he finds peace and happiness in his heart. I have forgiven myself for my part in the marriage. I know we both did the best we could with what we had.

My life has changed dramatically since my divorce. I am not the same person I was back then. I am truly a woman giving birth to myself. I know who I am and what I want. I know I can have what I want and deserve good in my life. I've needed these last ten years to be alone, to find myself, and fall in love with myself.

Last year, my first book was published, *Simply a Woman of Faith*. My book is about the power of prayer—asking for what you want and believing you will get it. It took seven years to write the book. I spent seven long years agonizing over it because I didn't believe in myself. I constantly told myself, "You are not a writer, you are wasting your time, and nobody will read it." I needed to change my thinking before anything would manifest on the outside.
I visualized and saw *Simply a Woman of Faith* in my hands before it was ever published, and I am happy to say that my book has been very successful so far. I am retiring from my job of twenty years in social services to promote and market my book, as well as lead spiritual retreats and workshops. A whole new world has opened up to me because I said "yes" to God and trusted the process and plan.

As I reflect on the ten years prior to getting a divorce, I realize now that I was quietly preparing myself by getting stronger spiritually, emotionally, and financially. I learned to take care of myself, stand up for myself, believe in myself, and love myself. I am grateful for the thirty years of marriage and the many lessons I learned. I understand that I cannot fix anyone else and that I alone am responsible for my life and happiness. Today, I counsel women and help them believe and love themselves.

It's a wonderful life and I look forward to the next chapter—when my soulmate appears. It's God's promise; I believe it and so it is.

Unending Praise for Making Love Visible

"June takes us on a remarkable journey into self-awareness, self-discovery, and most importantly, self-love. Her insight and depth of understanding in her book *The Benefit of the Ex* goes beyond just the subject of divorce, but into every part of life that brings challenges, separation, and disappointment. She teaches us to go inward for the answers we seek. The richness of this book is a must read!"

Juliet Carlson
Extras Casting Director

"Thanks, June! You've created a breakthrough moment for me and many others who will read *The Benefit of the Ex*. Benefiting from my ex never entered my consciousness until I read this wonderful book. It is a game changer in how we normally view divorce. You've moved the ball for all of us."

Willie Jones
World Champion of Public Speaking

"This is a great gift for anyone who has a broken heart that they think won't ever mend."

Lyla B. Berg, Ph.D.
Author, *Leaving the Gilded Cage*

"June Dillinger truly *makes love visible* in everything that she does. *The Benefit of the Ex* invites in new ways of being when we think love is no longer possible. I am grateful for the awakening experience these true stories have instilled in both my professional and personal life."

CJ Rice
State of Hawaii Crisis Prevention

Made in the USA
San Bernardino, CA
12 May 2020